Bell 76 - 99009   MAY 4 '70

THE SINO-SOVIET DISPUTE

KEESING'S RESEARCH REPORT

THE
SINO-SOVIET
DISPUTE

CHARLES SCRIBNER'S SONS
New York

CONTENTS

v

INTRODUCTION

This report, written by the editorial staff of *Keesing's Contemporary Archives,* traces relations between the Soviet Union and Communist China since the establishment of the People's Republic of China in 1949. It shows how, after the Treaty of Friendship, Alliance and Mutual Assistance of 1950 and the subsequent period of cooperation, differences between the two countries arose after Khrushchev's accession to power; what the ideological controversy on the nature and aims of present-day Communism is about; how it gradually led to increasingly bitter polemics; what territorial and border disputes exist; and what armed clashes have led up to the present confrontation.

The report, which includes extensive quotations from documents, is based on material published in the *Archives* from time to time, and also on information which has subsequently become available. The object of the report, as of the *Archives,* is to record the facts without comment as objectively as possible.

I: THE PERIOD OF FRIENDSHIP AND CO-OPERATION, 1949–55

The People's Republic of China was formally inaugurated on Oct. 1, 1949, and was officially recognized by the Soviet Union on the following day. The Communist seizure of power had been undertaken against the Soviet Government's advice; Mao Tse-tung revealed in 1962 that Stalin had warned the Chinese Communists in 1945 not to start a civil war, and had advised them to co-operate with the Kuomintang regime.

Treaty of Friendship and Other Agreements
(February 1950)

Mao Tse-tung, then Chairman (President) of the Chinese People's Republic, arrived in Moscow on an official visit on Dec. 16, 1949, and was joined by Chou En-lai, the Chinese Prime Minister and Foreign Minister, on Jan. 20, 1950. Negotiations between the two Governments terminated on Feb. 14 with the signature of (1) a treaty of friendship, alliance, and mutual assistance; (2) an agreement providing that after the signing of a peace treaty with Japan, and in any case not later than the end of 1952, the Soviet Union would transfer free of charge to the Chinese Government all its rights in the joint administration of the Manchurian (Changchun) Railway, together with the property belonging to the railway, and would withdraw its troops from the Port Arthur naval base, whose installations would be handed over to China; (3) an agreement on the granting of long-term credits to the amount of 300,000,000 U.S. dollars by the U.S.S.R. to China, to enable China to obtain industrial, mining, and railway equipment from the U.S.S.R. The provisions of the treaty of friendship and alliance were as follows:

Art. 1. China and the U.S.S.R. would take jointly "all the necessary measures at their disposal for the purpose of preventing a repetition of aggression and violation of the peace on the part of Japan or any State uniting with Japan, directly or indirectly, in acts of aggression." Should either China or the U.S.S.R. be attacked by Japan, or States allied with that country, the other party would immediately render military and other assistance with all the means at its disposal. Both China and the U.S.S.R. "declare their readiness, in a spirit of sincere co-operation, to participate in all international actions aimed at ensuring peace and security throughout the world, and will do all in their power to achieve the speediest implementation of these tasks."

Art. 2. China and the U.S.S.R. undertook "by means of mutual agreement to strive for the earliest conclusion of a peace treaty with Japan, jointly with the other Powers which were allies during the Second World War."

Art. 3. Both parties undertook not to conclude any alliance directed against the other, or to take part in "any coalition or in acts and measures" directed against the other.

Art. 4. Both parties would "consult each other in regard to all important international problems affecting the common interests of the Soviet Union and China, being guided by the interests of the consolidation of peace and universal security."

Art. 5. Both parties undertook "in a spirit of friendship and in conformity with the principles of equality and mutual respect for sovereignty, territorial integrity, and non-interference in the affairs of the other party, to develop and consolidate economic and cultural ties between the Soviet Union and China, to render each other all possible economic assistance, and to carry out the necessary economic co-operation."

Art. 6. The treaty would come into force on exchange of instruments of ratification (to take place in Peking), and would be valid for 30 years. Should neither party give notice of its intention to denounce the treaty one year before the term of its expiration, it would remain in force for another five years, and would be extended thereafter in conformity with this procedure. The treaty was drawn up in Russian and Chinese, both texts having equal validity.

2

An official announcement said that the negotiations had "proceeded in an atmosphere of cordiality and friendly mutual agreement," and had "confirmed the desire of both parties to strengthen and develop in every way relations of friendship and co-operation between them." Mao Tse-tung stated in 1962, however, that Stalin had held up the signing of the treaty of alliance for two months because he feared that the Chinese Communists, like the Yugoslav Communists, would pursue an independent policy, and that he had not begun to trust them until after the Korean War.

Under the economic aid agreement, 50 Chinese enterprises were built or renovated with the aid of Soviet experts. Joint Sino-Soviet companies were set up for mining certain metals in Sinkiang, for the extraction and refining of oil in that province, for the construction and repair of naval vessels at Dairen, and for the operation of civil airlines.

Chinese Membership of the United Nations

The Soviet delegate to the Security Council proposed unsuccessfully on Aug. 1, 1950, that China should be represented in the United Nations by the Communist instead of the Kuomintang regime, which had been transferred to Taiwan (Formosa). The proposal has since been repeatedly revived in the General Assembly, the last occasion being on Nov. 19, 1968, each time without success. Despite their subsequent differences, the U.S.S.R. has consistently supported Communist China's admission to the United Nations.

The Korean War—Soviet Military Aid to China (1950–53)

The Korean War began on June 25, 1950, and on Oct. 25, when the U.N. forces were rapidly advancing towards the Chinese frontier, Chinese troops entered Korea. During the war the U.S.S.R. supplied China with military aid to the value (according to U.S. estimates) of $2,000,000,000, including about 1,000 *Mig-15* aircraft and aid to war industries in Manchuria and the Chinese transport system. The modernization and mechanization of the Chinese armed forces with Soviet aid continued after the armistice of July 27, 1953, which ended the war. The Chinese produced heavy artillery and tanks copied from Soviet models, and later began producing *Migs* under Soviet licence, whilst the small Chinese Navy was equipped with submarines, at first supplied by the U.S.S.R., later produced in China.

Transfer of Soviet Rights in Manchurian Railway to China —Extension of Joint Control of Port Arthur (September 1952)

After talks in Moscow lasting nearly a month between Soviet leaders and a Chinese mission led by Chou En-lai, the Tass agency announced on Sept. 15, 1952, that the transfer of the Manchurian Railway would be completed by the end of the year, as agreed in 1950, but that at the Chinese Government's request the withdrawal of Soviet troops from Port Arthur would be postponed until Japan had concluded peace treaties with China and the U.S.S.R.

Increased Soviet Economic Aid to China (September 1953)

When Stalin died on March 5, 1953, he was succeeded as Prime Minister by Mr. Malenkov and as general secretary of the Communist Party by Mr. Khrushchev. The new Soviet regime greatly increased economic aid to China; a letter from Mao Tse-tung to Mr. Malenkov, published on Sept. 15, revealed that the Soviet Government had promised to "extend systematic economic and technical aid in the construction and renovation of 91 new enterprises in China and to the 50 enterprises now being built or renovated."

Restoration of Port Arthur to China—Further Increases in Soviet Aid (October 1954)

During 1953–55 a struggle for power was in progress between Mr. Malenkov and Mr. Khrushchev, in which the latter apparently sought and obtained Chinese support. He arrived in Peking on Sept. 29, 1954, for the celebrations of the fifth anniversary of the establishment of the Chinese People's Republic, at the head of a delegation which also included Marshal Bulganin (then the Soviet Defence Minister). At the conclusion of his visit it was announced on Oct. 12 that the following agreements had been reached:

(1) In view of the changed situation in the Far East caused by the ending of the Korean War, the establishment of peace in Indo-China by the Geneva Agreements, and the strengthening of China's defence potential, all Soviet troops would be evacuated from Port Arthur by May 31, 1955, and the installations would be transferred to China without compensation.

(2) The U.S.S.R. would grant China a long-term credit of 520,000,000 roubles; the U.S.S.R. would aid China in building 15 new industrial undertakings, and would increase deliveries of equipment for the 141 enterprises covered by the earlier agreements; and a joint commission of Soviet and Chinese technicians and scientists would meet at least twice a year to discuss Soviet technical aid to China. The U.S.S.R. would hand over to China on Jan. 1, 1955, all her shares in the joint Sino-Soviet companies, the value of which would be refunded in goods over a number of years.

(3) Two new railways linking China and the U.S.S.R. would be built, one running from Alma Ata (in the Soviet Republic of Kazakhstan) via the Chinese province of Sinkiang to Lanchow (in north-west China), whilst the second would run from Tinmin (in northern China) to Ulan Bator (in Outer Mongolia), which was already connected by rail with the Trans-Siberian Railway. The Chinese and Soviet Governments would be responsible for building the sections of the first railway in their respective territories, and Outer Mongolia would co-operate with the U.S.S.R. in building the second.

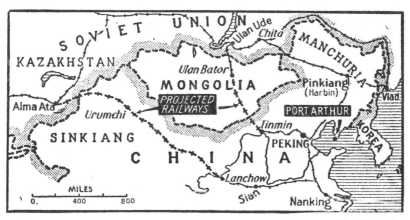

The Economist

Atomic Co-operation Agreement (May 1955)

Mr. Malenkov resigned the Premiership on March 8, 1955, and was succeeded by Marshal Bulganin, who said in one of his first official statements that "China can count in all circumstances on the aid of the U.S.S.R." Moscow Radio announced on May 1 that an agreement with China had been signed on Soviet aid in atomic research for peaceful purposes. It was stated that the agreement provided for (1) the completion of the necessary preparatory work in 1955–56 and the supply of experimental atomic piles and accelerators; (2) the free supply of scientific and technical information required for the installation of this apparatus, and the loan of Soviet specialists; (3) the supply of sufficient quantities of fissile material and radioactive isotopes until China was able to keep its atomic piles working without further Soviet aid; (4) the training of Chinese in nuclear physics.

II: THE BEGINNINGS OF DISAGREEMENT, 1956–59

Sino-Soviet friendship and co-operation reached its highest point during the period from 1953 to 1956, between the death of Stalin and Mr. Khrushchev's announcement of the de-Stalinization policy at the 20th congress of the Soviet Communist Party in February 1956. During the next four years the two countries gradually drifted apart, largely as a result of their differences on foreign policy, although these were not made public at the time.

The 20th Congress of the Soviet Communist Party (February 1956)

In his report to the 20th congress of the Soviet Communist Party, held on Feb. 14–25, 1956, Mr. Khrushchev reaffirmed the Soviet party's support for a policy of peaceful coexistence between countries with different social and political systems; rejected Lenin's theory that war was inevitable so long as capitalism existed; and held that in certain countries the transition to Socialism might take place peacefully by parliamentary means.

"The forces of peace," Mr. Khrushchev said, had been "considerably augmented by the emergence in the world of a group of peace-loving European

7

and Asian States which have proclaimed non-participation in blocs as a principle of their foreign policies." As a result, "a vast zone of peace has emerged in the world, including peace-loving States, both Socialist and non-Socialist, of Europe and Asia. This zone embraces vast areas inhabited by nearly 1,500,000,000 people—that is, the majority of the population of our planet."

"Under the impact of these incontestable facts," Mr. Khrushchev continued, "symptoms of a certain sobering-up are appearing among influential Western circles. More and more people in these circles are realizing what a dangerous gamble war against the Socialist countries may prove for the development of capitalism. . . . Nor is it a coincidence that prominent leaders of bourgeois countries with increasing frequency frankly admit that 'there will be no victor' in a war in which atomic weapons are used. . . .'"

On relations with the U.S.A. he said: "The establishment of firm friendly relations between the two biggest Powers of the world, the Soviet Union and the U.S.A. would be of great significance for the strengthening of world peace. If the well-known 'five principles of peaceful coexistence' were to underlie the relations between the Soviet Union and the U.S.A., it would be of truly great importance for all mankind. . . . These principles—mutual respect for territorial integrity and sovereignty, non-aggression, non-interference in one another's domestic affairs, equality and mutual advantage, peaceful co-existence and economic co-operation—are now subscribed to by a score of States. . . . We want to be friends with the U.S.A. and co-operate with it for peace and international security, and also in the economic and cultural spheres. We propose this with good intentions, without holding a knife behind our back. . . .'"

Enlarging on the Soviet attitude to peaceful co-existence, he said: "It has been alleged that the Soviet Union puts forward the principle of peaceful coexistence merely out of tactical considerations—considerations of expediency. But it is common knowledge that we have always, from the very first years of Soviet power, stood with equal firmness for peaceful coexistence. Hence it is not a tactical move, but a fundamental principle of Soviet foreign policy. . . . It goes without saying that among Communists there are no supporters of capitalism. But this does not mean that we have interfered, or plan to interfere, in the internal affairs of countries where capitalism exists. . . .

"When we say that the Socialist system will win in the competition between the two systems, the capitalist and the Socialist, this by no means signifies that its victory will be achieved through armed interference by the Socialist countries in the internal affairs of the capitalist countries. Our certainty of the victory of Communism is based on the fact that the Socialist mode of production possesses decisive advantages over the capitalist mode of production. . . . We have always held, and continue to hold, that the establishment of a new social system in this or that country is the internal affair of the people of the country concerned. . . . The principle of peaceful coexistence is gaining ever wider international recognition. . . . And this is natural, for in present-day conditions there is no other way out. Indeed, there are only two ways: either peaceful coexistence or the most destructive war in history. There is no third way."

The "Inevitability of War." Discussing whether a third world war was inevitable, Mr. Khrushchev said: "There is, of course, a Marxist-Leninist precept that wars are inevitable as long as imperialism exists. This precept was evolved at a time when imperialism was an all-embracing world system, and the social

8

and political forces which did not want war were weak, poorly organized, and thus unable to compel the imperialists to renounce war. . . . At the present time, however, the situation has radically changed. Now there is a world camp of Socialism which has become a mighty force. In this camp the peace forces find not only the moral but also the material means to prevent aggression. Moreover, there is a large group of other countries, with a population running into hundreds of millions, which is actively working to avert war. The labour movement in the capitalist countries has today become a tremendous force. The movement of peace supporters has sprung up and developed into a powerful factor.

"In these circumstances the Leninist precept certainly remains in force that, so long as imperialism exists, the economic basis giving rise to wars will continue to exist. That is why we must display the greatest vigilance. As long as capitalism survives in the world, the reactionary forces representing the interests of the capitalist monopolies will continue their drive towards military gambles and aggression, and may try to unleash war. But war is not fatalistically inevitable. Today there are mighty social and political forces possessing formidable means to prevent the imperialists from unleashing war, and, if they actually do try to start it, to deliver a smashing rebuff to the aggressors and frustrate their adventurist plans."

Forms of Transition to Socialism. After declaring that the transition to Socialism might take a number of forms, Mr. Khrushchev quoted a saying of Lenin that "All nations will arrive at Socialism, but not all will do so in exactly the same way," and observed that this saying had been confirmed by the experience of history. "It is probable that more forms of transition to Socialism will appear," he continued. "Moreover, the implementation of these forms need not be associated with civil war. The greater or lesser degree of intensity which the struggle may assume, the use or the non-use of violence in the transition to Socialism, depends on the resistance of the exploiters—on whether the exploiting class itself resorts to violence, rather than on the proletariat.

"In this connexion," Mr. Khrushchev went on, "the question arises whether it is possible to make the transition to Socialism by parliamentary means. No such course was open to the Russian Bolsheviks, who were the first to effect this transition. . . . Since then, however, the historical situation has undergone radical changes which make possible a new approach to the question. . . . The present situation offers the working class in a number of capitalist countries a real opportunity to unite the overwhelming majority of the people under its leadership and to secure the transfer of the basic means of production into the hands of the people. . . . The winning of a stable parliamentary majority backed by a mass revolutionary movement of the proletariat and all the working people could create for the working class of a number of capitalist and former colonial countries the conditions needed to secure fundamental social changes. In the countries where capitalism is still strong and has a huge military and police apparatus at its disposal, the reactionary forces will, of course, inevitably offer serious resistance. There the transition to Socialism will be attended by a sharp revolutionary struggle."

At a secret session of the congress Mr. Khrushchev made a long speech in which he denounced Stalin's wholesale executions of innocent people, the extraction of confessions by torture, his strategy in the Second World War, his responsibility for the breach with Yugoslavia in 1948, and the "personality cult" surrounding him.

Mr. Khrushchev's advocacy of peaceful coexistence did not mark in any sense a new departure in Soviet policy, nor was it incompatible with the views on international relations put forward by the Chinese Government at that time. At the 19th Communist Party congress in October 1952, at which Stalin was present, Mr. Malenkov said: "The Soviet policy of peace and security of the nations is based on the premise that the peaceful coexistence and co-operation of capitalism and Communism are quite possible, provided there is a mutual desire to co-operate, readiness to carry out commitments, and adherence to the principle of equal rights and non-interference in the internal affairs of other States. The Soviet Union has always stood for, and advocates, the development of trade and co-operation with other countries irrespective of the difference in social systems. . . . We have not the least intention of forcing our ideology or our economic system upon anybody. 'The export of revolution is nonsense. Every country will make its own revolution if it wants to, and if it does not want to there will be no revolution,' says Comrade Stalin. . . ."

The five principles of peaceful coexistence, to which Mr. Khrushchev referred in his report, were first formulated in an agreement between China and India signed on April 29, 1954. At the Bandung Conference of Afro-Asian countries, held in April 1955, Chou En-lai supported a resolution calling for the total prohibition of the manufacture of nuclear weapons and universal disarmament, and issued the following statement on relations between China and the U.S.A.: "The Chinese people are friendly to the American people. They do not want a war with the United States. The Chinese Government is willing to sit down and enter into negotiations with the U.S. Government to discuss the question of relaxing tension in the Far East, especially in the Formosa area."

The new features of Mr. Khrushchev's report were his rejection of the theory of the inevitability of war under capitalism and his acceptance of the possibility of a peaceful transition to Socialism. Although these theories, together with his denunciation of Stalin, were later to become the subject of bitter controversy between the Soviet and Chinese Communist parties, they were not publicly questioned at the time by the Chinese party, which endorsed his criticisms of Stalin in a statement issued on April 5, 1956.

Chinese Intervention in the Polish and Hungarian Crises
(October–November 1956)

Mr. Khrushchev's repudiation of Stalin's policies had profound repercussions throughout Eastern Europe, which in Poland and still more in Hungary assumed the form of open revolt against the Stalinist system. The central committee of the Polish United Workers' Party, at a session on Oct. 19–21, elected a new Politburo from which Stalinists were excluded and chose Mr. Gomulka, who had recently been released from prison, as its first secretary. Mr. Khrushchev and other Soviet leaders flew to Warsaw on Oct. 19, and Soviet tank formations began to move on Warsaw; the Polish leadership stood firm, however, and on Oct. 23 Mr. Khrushchev gave an assurance that all Soviet troops in Poland would return to their bases. In later official statements the Chinese party revealed that it had intervened in this crisis, and had advised the Soviet leaders against using force, and also against calling an international Communist conference to condemn the Polish party.

An armed revolt in Hungary in the last week of October was followed by the establishment on Oct. 30 of a four-party Government, which announced the discontinuation of the one-party system. The Soviet Government announced on the same day its readiness to withdraw its forces from Budapest, but on Nov. 4 the Soviet Army attacked Budapest, suppressed the national uprising by force, and installed a new Government headed by Mr. Kadar. Later Chinese statements revealed that this reversal of policy had been carried out on Chinese advice, and alleged that Mr. Khrushchev had adopted a vacillating attitude and had only with great difficulty been persuaded by the Chinese Government to "go to the defence of the Hungarian revolution."

Chou En-lai arrived in Moscow on Jan. 7, 1957, for discussions with the Soviet leaders; visited Warsaw on Jan. 11–16 and Budapest on Jan. 16–17; and returned to Moscow on Jan. 17 to resume his discussions. A joint statement issued by Marshal Bulganin and Chou En-lai on Jan. 18 called for the replacement of military alliances by collective security pacts for Europe and Asia and an agreement between the great Powers on disarmament, and claimed that attempts by both the U.S.S.R. and China to establish peaceful coexistence with the U.S.A. had been frustrated by "the claims of American monopoly circles for world domination and their policy of aggression and war preparations." The statement condemned the Hungarian uprising as "provoked by imperialist aggressive quarters and Hungarian counter-revolutionary elements" in order to "destroy the Socialist system in Hungary, restore Fascist dictatorship, and thereby create a hotbed of war in Europe," and described its suppression as "a major victory for the cause of peace and Socialism." It affirmed the principle of complete equality between Socialist countries, and stated that "it is fully possible in their relations to combine the unity of Socialist countries and the independence of each individual country."

Secret Agreement on Nuclear Armament of China (October 1957)

Under a secret agreement signed on Oct. 15, 1957, the U.S.S.R. undertook to supply the necessary scientific information and technical materials to enable China to manufacture its own nuclear weapons. This agreement was never carried out, and its existence was revealed by China only in 1963.

The 12-Nation Moscow Declaration (November 1957)

Delegations from all the Communist countries visited Moscow in November 1957 for the celebrations of the 40th anniversary of the Bolshevik Revolution, the Chinese delegation being headed by Mao Tse-tung. During the celebrations representatives of the ruling parties of all the 13 Communist countries except Yugoslavia met on Nov. 14–16 for discussions, at the conclusion of which they issued a lengthy joint declaration. In a speech to the conference, which later aroused much controversy, Mao Tse-tung said that there was a possibility of preventing another world war, but even if nuclear war broke out at least half the world's population would survive, and "the whole world would become Socialist."

The declaration reaffirmed the principle of peaceful coexistence and the possibility of achieving Socialism through parliamentary

12

means, and condemned both "revisionism" and "dogmatism." According to later Chinese statements, however, in its final form it incorporated significant amendments on which the Chinese party had insisted.

The declaration stated that the 12 parties adhered to the "Leninist principle of peaceful coexistence . . . which . . . coincides with the Five Principles put forward jointly by China and India and with the programme adopted at the Bandung conference of Afro-Asian countries."

On "dogmatism" and "revisionism" the declaration said: "In condemning dogmatism, the Communist parties believe that the main danger at present is revisionism—in other words, right-wing opportunism as a manifestation of bourgeois ideology paralyzing the revolutionary energy of the working-class and demanding the preservation or restoration of capitalism. However, dogmatism and sectarianism can also be the main danger at different phases of development in one party or another. It is for each Communist party to decide what danger threatens it more at a given time. . . . Modern revisionism seeks to smear the teaching of Marxism-Leninism, declares that it is 'outmoded,' and alleges that it has lost its significance for social progress. . . . The revisionists deny the historical necessity for a proletarian revolution and the dictatorship of the proletariat during the period of transition from capitalism to socialism; reject the principles of proletarian internationalism; and call for the rejection of the Leninist principles of party organization and democratic centralism. Above all, they call for the transformation of the Communist party from a militant revolutionary party into some kind of debating society. . . .

"The working class and its vanguard—the Marxist-Leninist party—seek to achieve the Socialist revolution by peaceful means," the declaration continued. "In a number of capitalist countries the working-class today has the opportunity—given a united working-class and people's front, or other workable forms of political co-operation between the different parties and organizations—to unite a majority of the people, win power without civil war, and ensure the transfer of the basic means of production to the hands of the people . . . [The] . . . working-class . . . can secure a firm majority in parliament, transform parliament from an instrument serving the class interests of the bourgeoisie into an instrument serving the working people, launch a non-parliamentary mass struggle, smash the resistance of the reactionary forces, and create the necessary conditions for the peaceful realization of the Socialist revolution . . . .

"In the event of the ruling classes resorting to violence against the people, the possibility of non-peaceful transition to Socialism should be borne in mind. Leninism teaches, and experience confirms, that the ruling classes never relinquish power voluntarily. In this case the degree of bitterness and the forms of the class struggle will depend not so much on the proletariat as on the resistance put up by the reactionary circles . . ." The possibility of one or another way to Socialism depends on the concrete conditions in each country . . . .

[The term "revisionism" was originally applied to the teachings of the German Social Democrat Eduard Bernstein, who in 1898 put forward the view that Marx's theories should be revised in view of subsequent political and economic developments; hence it is applied by Communists to theories

13

which are considered to depart from the fundamental principles of Marxism. The terms "dogmatism" and "sectarianism" are used of ultra-leftist doctrines and policies which fail to take the practical realities of the existing political situation into account.]

A Peace Manifesto, calling for the complete prohibition of nuclear weapons, the ending of the arms race and military blocs, and support for a policy of peaceful coexistence, was signed by representatives of all the 64 Communist parties taking part in the celebrations, including the Chinese party.

The Yugoslav League of Communists neither participated in the 12-party discussions nor signed the declaration, although it did sign the Peace Manifesto. Mr. Kardelj, who had led the Yugoslav delegation at the celebrations, said on returning to Belgrade that "we did not sign it because we did not agree with it." Relations between the Soviet and Yugoslav Communist parties drastically deteriorated in 1958, when a new programme adopted by the League of Communists was attacked in the Soviet Press, and still more violently in the Chinese Press, for its "revisionist" character.

The Middle Eastern Crisis (July–August 1958)

The fundamental differences between China and the U.S.S.R. on questions of international policy first became apparent in the summer of 1958. Following the Iraqi revolution of July 14, President Chamoun of Lebanon appealed to President Eisenhower to send U.S. forces to that country, and King Hussein of Jordan made a similar appeal to Britain; in consequence U.S. Marines landed in Lebanon on July 15, and British parachute troops arrived in Jordan two days later. In a letter to President Eisenhower, Mr. Khrushchev (who had succeeded Marshal Bulganin as Prime Minister in March) proposed on July 19 an immediate conference of the Heads of Government of the U.S.S.R., the U.S.A., Britain, France, and India. President Eisenhower in his reply proposed on July 22 that such a meeting should take place within the framework of the U.N. Security Council, and this suggestion was accepted by Mr. Khrushchev on the following day.

Mr. Khrushchev visited Peking from July 31 to Aug. 3 for talks with the Chinese leaders. The communiqué issued at the conclusion

14

of the talks referred to the "complete identity of views" between the two Governments; condemned the U.S. and British "aggression" in Lebanon and Jordan; and called for an immediate conference of Heads of Government and the immediate withdrawal of the U.S. and British troops from Lebanon and Jordan. It also said that the two Communist parties would "wage an uncompromising struggle against revisionism—the principal danger in the Communist movement," which had found its clearest manifestation in the programme of the Yugoslav League of Communists.

On the question of war and peace the communiqué said: "The Soviet Union and the Chinese People's Republic will do everything possible to ease international tension and prevent the horrors of a new war. Both parties declare once again that the right of the peoples of all countries to choose their own social and political systems must be respected; that countries with different social systems must co-exist peacefully, in accordance with the well-known 'Five Principles' which have received wide international recognition; that all controversial international issues must be settled peacefully by negotiation; and that the development of economic and cultural relations between countries on the basis of mutual benefit and peaceful competition . . . must be encouraged.

"The major task in preserving and consolidating peace is the reaching of agreement among States to reduce armaments, to end [nuclear] tests and ban atomic and hydrogen weapons, to abolish all military groupings and bases on foreign territories, and to conclude a pact of peace and collective security. Whether war can be averted does not, however, depend solely on the good intentions of the peace-loving peoples and their unilateral efforts. Right up to the present moment, aggressive circles of the Western Powers are refusing to take any genuine measures to preserve peace; on the contrary, they are senselessly aggravating the international tension and putting mankind on the brink of catastrophe. If the sabre-rattling imperialist maniacs dare to force war on the peoples, they should realize that all the peace-loving and freedom-loving countries, closely united in a single unit, will put an end to the imperialist aggressors once and for all and establish everlasting peace the world over."

After returning to Moscow Mr. Khrushchev again wrote to President Eisenhower on Aug. 5, withdrawing his support for the proposed summit meeting on the ground that the Security Council was dominated by the U.S.A. and its allies, and demanding the admission of the Chinese People's Republic to the United Nations. His *volte-face* was believed to be a direct result of his discussions in Peking.

In his letter Mr. Khrushchev said *inter alia*: "If we glance at the composition of the Security Council as it now stands, we are bound to draw the conclusion that . . . this body has become a kind of committee dominated by member-countries of NATO, the Baghdad Pact, and SEATO, a committee in

15

which the lawful seat of the great Chinese People's Republic is held by a representative of a political corpse—Chiang Kai-shek.

"The policy of ignoring People's China is sheer madness. This great Power exists and is growing stronger, regardless of whether or not it is recognized by certain Governments . . . Without the Chinese People's Republic, the Security Council and the U.N. cannot be completely effective bodies in safeguarding peace and ensuring security . . . A situation has thus arisen in which the Security Council has in fact been paralyzed and is unable to take, against the will of the United States, any decision which would effectively promote the safeguarding of world peace . . ."

The Quemoy Crisis (August–October 1958)

On Aug. 23 the Chinese Army began an almost daily bombardment of the offshore island of Quemoy, which was held by the Kuomintang forces. Mr. John Foster Dulles (then the U.S. Secretary of State) declared on Sept. 4 that U.S. forces would be used for the protection of Quemoy, and by the middle of the month a powerful U.S. air and naval force had been assembled in the Western Pacific. Mr. Khrushchev warned President Eisenhower on Sept. 8 that "an attack on the Chinese People's Republic, which is a great friend, ally, and neighbour of our country, is an attack on the Soviet Union," whilst stressing his wish to "find a common language with you" so that the parties concerned might "join their efforts in removing the tension which has arisen in the Far East." President Eisenhower replied on Sept. 13, accusing the Chinese Government of "aggression." In a Note of Sept. 19, which was formally rejected by the U.S. Government, Mr. Khrushchev contended that U.S. support for the Kuomintang Government was responsible for the crisis, and that there could be no lasting peace in the Far East until the U.S. armed forces were recalled from Formosa and the Formosa Straits. Tension in the area relaxed after the Chinese Government temporarily suspended the bombardment of Quemoy on Oct. 6.

Mao Tse-tung revealed in September 1962 that Mr. Khrushchev proposed at this time that China and the U.S.S.R. should form a joint war fleet. This proposal was rejected by the Chinese leaders, who, according to Mao, regarded it as an attempt by the U.S.S.R. to control the Chinese coast and to facilitate an eventual blockade of China.

The Communes and the "Great Leap Forward" (1958)

Between April and August the movement for the grouping of agricultural co-operatives into large people's communes combining small-scale industry with agriculture swept China. The Communist Party Politburo formally approved the movement in August, and at the same time approved the "Great Leap Forward" policy for the rapid industrialization of China, the target for steel production for 1958 being raised to 10,700,000 tons, compared with 5,900,000 tons produced in 1957. For this purpose the party abandoned its previous policy of relying for its industrial output primarily on large industrial complexes built with Soviet aid and requiring several years to construct, and instead adopted a policy of constructing hundreds of thousands of small and medium plants all over China.

The Chinese Government's new economic policy was not approved by the Communist Party in the U.S.S.R. where the Press and radio were extremely reticent in their references to it. The *Washington Post* reported on Dec. 17 that at a recent meeting with Senator Hubert Humphrey Mr. Khrushchev had described the commune system as "reactionary" and inappropriate for the U.S.S.R.

The central committee of the Chinese party, meeting from Nov. 28 to Dec. 10, approved a proposal by Mao Tse-tung that he should resign the post of Chairman of the Republic, while remaining chairman of the party, in order to concentrate on theoretical work. It was widely suggested that he had been forced to resign because of the failure of the communes, the plan to double steel production, and Chinese policy on the offshore islands. A resolution adopted at the same time said that industrialization would take a very long time; that the transition from Socialism to Communism (i.e. from the principle of "to each according to his work" to that of "to each according to his needs") would take "fifteen, twenty, or more years, counting from now"; and that attempts to distribute supplies "according to need" were "an attempt to enter Communism by over-reaching ourselves—undoubtedly a Utopian concept that cannot succeed." Liu Shao-chi succeeded Mao as Chairman of the Republic in April 1959.

17

The 21st Soviet Party Congress (January–February 1959)

At the 21st Soviet Communist Party congress, held from Jan. 27 to Feb. 5, 1959, no open signs of tension between the U.S.S.R. and China appeared. In his report to the congress Mr. Khrushchev described "the aggressive policy of the U.S.A. towards the Chinese People's Republic and other peace-loving States" as the main source of tension in the Far East, and suggested the creation of an atom-free zone in the Far East and the Pacific. He also said that "the Communist Party of China is employing many original forms of Socialist construction, but we have no disagreements with it . . . We are in full and complete agreement with our brother party in China, though in many respects its methods of building Socialism do not resemble our own."

Chou En-lai, addressing the congress, spoke of the "eternal and unbreakable" friendship between the U.S.S.R. and China, and read a message from Mao Tse-tung praising Mr. Khrushchev's "correct leadership," but made no reference to the latter's proposal for an atom-free zone in the Far East.

The Peng Teh-huai Episode (May–September 1959)

During an official visit to Albania on May 25–June 4 Mr. Khrushchev met the Chinese Defence Minister, Marshal Peng Teh-huai. It was later revealed that at this meeting Marshal Peng showed him a memorandum strongly criticizing the Great Leap Forward and the communes, which he afterwards submitted to a meeting of the central committee of the Chinese party held in July and August. It was announced on Sept. 17 that he had been replaced as Defence Minister by Marshal Lin Piao. The new appointment marked a significant change in Chinese military policy, as Marshal Peng favoured close collaboration with the U.S.S.R. as the only possible source of modern weapons, whereas Marshal Lin was the leading advocate of the Maoist theory that manpower and morale rather than armaments are the decisive factors in war.

Soviet Repudiation of Agreement on Nuclear Weapons
(June 1959)

The U.S.S.R. repudiated on June 20 the secret agreement of 1957 on the supply of aid to China in manufacturing nuclear weapons. This reversal of policy, which was deeply resented by the Chinese and contributed to bring about the fall of Marshal Peng Teh-huai, was apparently motivated by Mr. Khrushchev's desire to achieve a rapprochement with the U.S.A., by his plan for an atom-free zone in the Far East, and by his distrust of the increasingly bellicose tendencies of China's foreign policy. A Chinese broadcast of Aug. 15, 1963, which first revealed details of the agreement, asserted that its repudiation was intended "as a gift for the Soviet leader to take to Eisenhower when visiting the U.S.A. in September."

The Longju Incident (August 1959)

A series of developments in the summer and autumn of 1959, arising from Mr. Khrushchev's attempts to improve relations with the U.S.A. and China's expansionist policy on the Indian frontier, brought the differences between the U.S.S.R. and China over foreign policy to a head. On Aug. 25–26 Chinese troops occupied the frontier post of Longju, which the Indian Government claimed was within the North-East Frontier Agency; Chou En-lai, however, maintained in a note to India that it was in Chinese territory and had been occupied by Indian troops.

A statement issued on Sept. 9 by the Tass Agency pointed out that the Soviet Union "maintains friendly relations with the Chinese People's Republic and the Republic of India"; that the Chinese and Soviet peoples were "linked by unbreakable bonds of fraternal friendship based on the great principles of socialist internationalism"; and that "friendly co-operation between the U.S.S.R. and India is developing successfully in keeping with the ideas of peaceful co-existence." It expressed confidence that China and India would settle their misunderstandings arising out of the "deplorable" frontier incidents, and declared that "attempts to exploit the incidents . . .

19

for the purpose of fanning the cold war . . . should be resolutely condemned." At the 1960 Moscow Conference [see below] Teng Hsiao-ping, general secretary of the Chinese Communist Party, declared that this "tendentious" communiqué first "revealed our differences to the world."

Mr. Khrushchev's Visit to U.S.A. (September 1959)

Mr. Khrushchev and Mr. Gromyko (the Soviet Foreign Minister) paid an official visit to the U.S.A. from Sept. 15 to Sept. 28, at the conclusion of which the former had three days of private talks with President Eisenhower at Camp David. In his public statements during the visit Mr. Khrushchev repeatedly emphasized the dangers of nuclear war, appealed for peaceful coexistence and universal and complete disarmament, and paid high tributes to President Eisenhower, and after returning to Moscow he expressed his conviction that the President "sincerely wants to liquidate the cold war and improve relations between our two great countries." His praise of President Eisenhower aroused particular anger in China; at the 1960 Moscow Conference Teng Hsiao-ping said that "no considerations of diplomatic protocol can explain away or excuse Khrushchev's tactless eulogy of Eisenhower and other imperialists."

Mr. Khrushchev's Visit to Peking (September–October 1959)

Immediately after returning from the U.S.A. Mr. Khrushchev and Mr. Gromyko flew to Peking for the celebrations of the tenth anniversary of the Chinese People's Republic. In their public statements the Chinese leaders abstained from criticism of Mr. Khrushchev's visit to the U.S.A.; at a banquet on Sept. 30 Chou En-lai congratulated him on "the success of his mission to the U.S.A. as an envoy of peace." In his reply Mr. Khrushchev emphasized that war must be precluded as a means of settling international disputes, gave a warning against "testing the capitalist system by force," and declared that "Socialism cannot be imposed by force of arms."

"The stronger the forces of the Socialist camp become, the more opportunities it will have for successfully upholding the cause of peace," Mr. Khrushchev said. "The forces of Socialism are already so great that concrete

20

possibilities are developing of precluding war as a means of settling international disputes. In our times the Heads of Government of some capitalist countries are beginning to show a certain tendency towards a realistic understanding of the situation existing in the world today. When I talked to President Eisenhower, my impression was that the President of the United States—and he has the support of many people—is aware of the need to relax international tension. . . . We, for our part, must do everything possible to preclude war as a means of settling outstanding questions. These questions must be solved through negotiations. . . . There is only one way to maintain peace—the way of peaceful co-existence of States with different social systems. . . .

"The Socialist countries," Mr. Khrushchev continued, "have the means of defence against the imperialist aggressors should the latter attempt to force them to leave the Socialist road by interference in their affairs. . . . That time has gone for ever. But . . . this certainly does not mean that since we are so strong we should test the stability of the capitalist system by force. That would be wrong; the peoples would never understand and would never support those who took it into their heads to act in this way. . . . Even such a noble and progressive system as Socialism cannot be imposed by force of arms against the will of the people. That is why Socialist countries, pursuing their consistent peace policy, concentrate on peaceful construction. . . . The question of when this or that country will embark on the Socialist road must be decided by the people themselves. This principle is sacrosanct for us. . . ."

While in Peking Mr. Khrushchev had a series of meetings with the Chinese leaders, but no communiqué was issued, suggesting that they had failed to reach agreement. Before leaving Peking on Oct. 4, Mr. Khrushchev made a short speech at the airport in which he reaffirmed his belief that it was possible to "rule out war for all time as a means of solving international disputes," and said that the Soviet Union would "take advantage of any possibilities in order to end the cold war."

The Ladakh Incident (October 1959)

A second serious incident on the Indian border occurred on Oct. 20–21, when nine members of an Indian police patrol were killed and 10 captured in a clash with Chinese troops. The Indian Government claimed that the incident took place 40 miles inside Ladakh (the northern region of Kashmir); the Chinese Government maintained that the Indians had intruded into Chinese territory.

Mr. Khrushchev said on Nov. 7 that the Soviet Government would "do everything to help" in finding a solution to the Sino-Indian frontier dispute, which should be settled amicably; as regards the

Ladakh incident, he said that the area was "uninhabited and not of any particular significance." The Soviet Press adopted a completely neutral attitude towards the incident, printing the Indian and Chinese versions side by side without comment.

Continued Soviet Economic Aid to China (1956–59)

Soviet economic and technical aid to China was continued throughout this period, the main agreements being as follows:

(1) An agreement signed on April 7, 1956, provided that 55 new factories and plants would be built in China with Soviet assistance, in addition to the 156 industrial enterprises stipulated under earlier Sino-Soviet agreements. The new installations to be built would include metallurgical, engineering, and chemical plants, factories to produce plastics and artificial fibres, electrotechnical and radio plants, power stations, an artificial liquid fuel plant, and aviation industry research institutes. The total cost of these installations would amount to about 2,500 million roubles (approx. $636,000,000 at nominal rates), which the Chinese Government would defray by supplying goods of various kinds to the Soviet Union.

(2) An agreement for the joint development of the Amur-Argun river basin, which forms the boundary between Manchuria and the Soviet Far East, was announced on Aug. 19, 1956. The plan provided for the building of a series of hydro-electric power stations, the industrial development of the area, and a new outlet for the Amur River, which is not deep enough for large ships and is frozen at its mouth for much of the year.

(3) An agreement signed on Aug. 8, 1958, provided for the construction or expansion of 47 metallurgical, chemical, coal-mining, machine-building, woodworking, and building materials enterprises and power stations.

(4) An agreement providing for additional Soviet financial and technical aid during the eight-year period 1959–67, which was signed on Feb. 7, 1959, envisaged the construction of 78 large enterprises, 31 more than in the previous agreement, which it superseded. The total amount of Soviet assistance under the agreement was given as 5,000,000,000 roubles (about $1,250,000,000), which China would repay by deliveries of goods.

(5) A protocol on scientific and technical co-operation was signed on Oct. 12, 1959, under which Soviet and Chinese institutions were to exchange specialists and technical information on metallurgy, machine-building, the coal and chemical industries, and other aspects of scientific research.

In a survey of this subject published on March 20, 1969, *Le Monde* stated: "The 141 'units' created with Russian aid [i.e. those announced in 1953]—factories, enterprises, dams, laboratories, development projects, etc.—gradually became 156 in 1954, then 211 in 1956, and finally about 250 in 1959. In many cases the Chinese merely built the factories from Russian plans, and the Russians

22

supplied all the machinery, directed its installation, set it going, and left only when production had begun. Chou En-lai has said that between 1949 and 1959 the U.S.S.R. supplied 10,800 technicians, in addition to whom 1,500 came from Central Europe. Between 1951 and 1957 the Russians claim to have trained 13,600 Chinese specialists, students, and workers in the U.S.S.R. The total amount of Soviet loans to China has never been revealed, but American experts have estimated it at $2,200,000,000, of which a little over $400,000,000 went to military aid and the rest to industrialization."

III: THE BEGINNING OF
OPEN CONTROVERSY, 1960–62

In April 1960 the Chinese party made public for the first time
its ideological differences with the Soviet party, although until the
end of 1962 both sides refrained from attacking each other directly.
The Chinese directed their attacks ostensibly against "revisionists"
in general and the Yugoslavs in particular, the Russians against
"dogmatists" in general and (after the breach with the Albanian
party in 1961) the Albanians in particular. The main issues in debate in the earlier stages of the controversy were as follows:

(1) The Chinese rejected as a "naïve illusion" Mr. Khrushchev's view that
war was no longer inevitable under capitalism, that disarmament was possible,
and that certain Western political leaders recognized the necessity of peaceful coexistence, and held that Mr. Khrushchev's foreign policy involved a
rejection of the class struggle and "peace at any price."

(2) As an argument in favour of peaceful coexistence, the Soviet party
emphasized that nuclear war would prove equally disastrous to all concerned. The Chinese party upheld Mao Tse-tung's view, as expressed at the
1957 Moscow Conference, that a third world war would result in further
victories for Communism.

(3) The U.S.S.R. was more cautious than China in assisting nationalist
movements in colonial and underdeveloped countries, in view of their possible repercussions on the international situation. Whereas, for example, the
Chinese recognized the Provisional Government set up by the Algerian na-
tionalists immediately after its formation in 1958, the Soviet Government

did not do so, apparently in order to avoid complications in its relations with France, and granted *de facto* recognition only in October 1960.

(4) Soviet theoreticians contended that in underdeveloped countries Communists should ally themselves with the "national bourgeoisie" in the struggle for national independence, which would prepare the way for the transition to Socialism; an example of this theory in practice was Stalin's advice to the Chinese Communists in 1945 to collaborate with the Kuomintang. *Pravda* emphasized on Aug. 26, 1960, that "high-handed treatment of anti-imperialist actions" not led by Communists constituted "a very dangerous form of sectarianism," and condemned the idea of "exporting revolution" and imposing on other countries social systems not developing from their internal conditions. In reply, the Peking *People's Daily* declared on Aug. 30 that "if we view the movement led by the bourgeoisie in colonial countries as the mainstream of the national liberation movement, and give full support to it while ignoring or expressing contempt for the anti-imperialist struggle waged by the revolutionary masses, it will in fact mean the adoption of bourgeois viewpoints."

(5) The Chinese party adopted a sceptical attitude towards Mr. Khrushchev's view that in certain circumstances it was possible for Communist parties to attain power by parliamentary means without violent revolution.

(6) The Soviet party held that China's nationalist foreign policy, as exemplified in its relations with India, seriously harmed the international Communist movement.

(7) The Chinese did not support the Soviet repudiation of the "personality cult" surrounding Stalin—largely, Soviet sources suggested, because Mao Tsetung had himself become the centre of a similar cult in China.

(8) The Chinese accused the Soviet party of seeking to impose its will on the world Communist movement; in 1956, for example, it had condemned Stalin and put forward the theories of the non-inevitability of war and the possibility of a peaceful transition to Socialism without previously consulting other Communist parties. The Soviet party retaliated by accusing the Chinese of splitting the movement by their "fractionalist" activities.

(9) The Soviet party upheld the accepted Marxist theory that intensive industrialization was an essential pre-requisite for the transition from Socialism to Communism, and regarded the communes as an attempt to "bypass certain historical stages." Chinese theoreticians, on the other hand, contended that agricultural expansion was "the one essential base."

(10) The Soviet Press laid increasing emphasis on the dangers of dogmatism and sectarianism, and since 1959 had relaxed its campaign against the Yugoslavs' alleged revisionism. The Chinese party, however, continued to uphold the assertion of the 1957 Moscow declaration that revisionism was "the main danger" to the international Communist movement.

The Beginning of the Controversy (April–June 1960)

The Chinese party journal *Red Flag* published on April 16, 1960, the first of a series of articles entitled *Long Live Leninism*, which forcefully stated the Chinese view on many of the issues in dispute. While accepting the principle of peaceful coexistence and holding that Communists must seek to avoid a major war, it maintained that the danger of such a war would remain as long as capitalism existed. It rejected the view that a nuclear war would destroy civilization, and declared that "on the ruins of destroyed imperialism the victorious peoples will create with tremendous speed a civilization a thousand times higher than the capitalist system, and will build their bright future." The articles also distinguished between major wars and local wars arising from revolutionary movements, which could only assist the progress of the revolution; quoted Lenin in support of the view that the transition to Socialism was impossible without revolutionary violence; and advocated that all revolutionary movements should be supported "resolutely and without the least reservation."

Soviet spokesmen speedily replied to this challenge. Mr. Otto Kuusinen (a member of the party Presidium) said in a speech on April 22 that there existed "a division in the ruling quarters of the imperialist States," and that "side by side with the hardened enemies of peace there appear sober-thinking statesmen who realize that a war fought with the new means of mass destruction would be madness." He went on to criticize those who held dogmatically to the view that imperialism was aggressive, and who failed to realize the need to make use of this new factor to save mankind from another war.

A number of pointed references to the controversy appeared in the Soviet Press in articles commemorating the 40th anniversary of the publication of Lenin's *"Left-Wing" Communism: An Infantile Disorder*, in which he criticized ultra-leftist Communists who refused to work in "reactionary" trade unions or to participate in "bourgeois" Parliaments, and emphasized the necessity of accepting compromises in certain circumstances. *Sovietskaya Rossiya* said on June 10 that "present-day leftists regard the policy of achieving peaceful coexistence, stopping the arms race, and friendship between the peoples of capitalist and Socialist countries as a retreat from Marxism-Leninism. They take the slightest deterioration in the international situation as proof of the correctness of their sectarian views." *Pravda* stated two days later that "we consider erroneous and incorrect the statements of leftists in the international Communist movement to the effect that, since we have taken power into our own hands, we can at once introduce Communism, by-passing certain historical stages in its development." *Kommunist* declared on June 23 that "the tendency of some political leaders to see the policy of peaceful coexistence and the struggle for disarmament as a retreat from Marxist-Leninist positions . . . and the desire to sow distrust for the decision of the 20th and 21st party congresses regarding the policy of averting a new war in present circumstances cannot be described otherwise than as being mistaken, dogmatic, and left-sectarian."

The Chinese Press in turn replied vigorously to these criticisms. *Red Flag* denounced on June 15 the "Yugoslav revisionists" who contended that "sober" and "sensible" imperialist politicians had "orientated themselves in the positive direction," and that this constituted "a new factor in the situation." The *People's Daily* asserted on June 25 that "so long as the monopoly capitalist clique continues its rule in the U.S.A. and American imperialism exists, the threat of war will not be eliminated and world peace will not be guaranteed," and denounced the "revisionists" who, "frightened out of their wits by imperialist blackmail of nuclear war, have exaggerated the consequences of such a war and have begged imperialism for peace at any cost."

The Bucharest Conference (June 1960)

In a letter of June 2 to the Chinese party, the Soviet party proposed an international meeting to resolve differences. The Chinese party agreed, but asked for time to prepare for it. The Soviet party suggested on June 7 that the forthcoming congress of the Romanian Workers' Party would provide the opportunity for a preliminary conference, to which the Chinese agreed.

Delegations from all the Communist countries of Europe and Asia except Yugoslavia attended the Romanian party congress, which was held in Bucharest from June 20 to June 25, the Soviet delegation being headed by Mr. Khrushchev and the Chinese delegation by Peng Chen, a member of the party's Politburo and Secretariat. Addressing the congress on June 21, Mr. Khrushchev reaffirmed the view that war was no longer inevitable, and defended his conduct at the abortive Summit Conference held in Paris on May 16–17.

"In present conditions," he said, "when there are two world systems, it is imperative to build mutual relations between them in such a way as to preclude the possibility of war breaking out. . . . One must bear in mind that the attitude to the question of peaceful co-existence is not everywhere the same in the imperialist countries. During the conversations I had in Paris with President de Gaulle and Prime Minister Macmillan, it seemed to me that they showed a certain understanding of the necessity for peaceful co-existence, and were even persuading themselves that the policy of co-existence must be the guiding principle in the future relations between States with different social systems. . . .

"We do not intend to yield to provocation and to deviate from the general line of our foreign policy, which . . . is one of coexistence, consolidating peace, easing international tension, and doing away with the cold war. The thesis that war is not inevitable in our time has a direct bearing on the policy of peaceful coexistence. . . . Lenin's propositions about imperialism remain in force, and are still a lodestar for us in our theory and practice. But it

27

should not be forgotten that Lenin's propositions on imperialism were advanced and developed decades ago. . . ."

Developing this latter point, Mr. Khrushchev continued: "The Soviet Union, with its enormous economic and military potential, is growing and gaining in strength. The great Socialist camp, which now numbers over 1,000,000,000 people, is growing and gaining in strength. The organization and political consciousness of the working-class have grown, and even in the capitalist countries it is actively fighting for peace. . . . One cannot mechanically repeat now on this question what Lenin said many decades ago on imperialism, and go on asserting that imperialist wars are inevitable until Socialism triumphs throughout the world. . . . History will possibly witness a time when capitalism is preserved only in a small number of States. . . . Even in such conditions, would one have to look up in a book what Lenin said, quite correctly for his time? Would one have to repeat that wars are inevitable since capitalist countries exist? . . . One cannot ignore the . . . changes in the correlation of forces in the world, and repeat what the great Lenin said in quite different historical conditions. . . ."

The speech of Peng Chen, who addressed the congress on June 22, was in striking contrast to that of Mr. Khrushchev. Whilst endorsing the 1957 Moscow Declaration, he declared that "as long as imperialism exists there will always be a danger of aggressive war," adding that war could be prevented only if the "Socialist camp" and the Afro-Asian and Latin American countries united. This, he declared, made it necessary to fight against the "revisionism" of "the Tito group, who are playing the imperialist game."

Private discussions meanwhile took place between the delegations. The Soviet delegation circulated on June 21 a letter containing a detailed criticism of the Chinese party's positions, which contended *inter alia* that the Chinese, after accepting that peaceful coexistence and a peaceful transition to Socialism were possible, had reversed their attitude; that to regard war as inevitable "paralyzed the revolutionary struggle" by inducing a spirit of despair; that coexistence did not involve the renunciation of national liberation movements; and that the Soviet party did not regard the "peaceful way" to Socialism as the only way, as the Chinese party had suggested. In the course of the discussions, which were often heated, Mr. Khrushchev was reported to have attacked Mao Tse-tung by name, calling him "an ultra-leftist, an ultra-dogmatist, indeed, a left revisionist," and to have accused China of "great-nation chauvinism" in its dealings with India.

A communiqué approved on June 24 reaffirmed the 12 parties' support for the 1957 declaration, including its statements on peaceful coexistence, the possibility of preventing wars, and the possibility of a peaceful transition to Socialism; also reaffirmed their support for the Peace Manifesto; and emphasized the need to strengthen "the unity of the countries of the world Socialist system." It was also agreed to convene a world Communist conference in Moscow. The central committee of the Soviet party, meeting on July 13–16, adopted a resolution approving the Soviet delegation's line at the Bucharest Conference, and condemning "dogmatic and left-wing sectarian deviations."

The Chinese party replied in detail to the Soviet letter of June 21 in a letter of Sept. 10, which contended *inter alia* that the conflict of views went back to the Soviet party congress of 1956, when the Soviet party had ignored Stalin's "positive role" and had put forward a false theory of "peaceful transition" without previously consulting the other Communist parties.

Withdrawal of Soviet Technical Aid to China (July–August 1960)

The Soviet Government informed the Chinese Government on July 16 of its decision to withdraw in August all Soviet technicians working in China. This unilateral decision, which aroused greater resentment in China than any other action of the Soviet Government, with the possible exception of the repudiation of the agreement on nuclear weapons, struck a crushing blow at China's economy at a time when the country was suffering from a series of natural disasters described by Peking Radio as "without parallel in the past century," including drought, typhoons, floods, and plagues of locusts and other insects. According to later Chinese statements, 1,390 experts were withdrawn, 343 contracts concerning technical aid cancelled, and 257 projects of scientific and technical co-operation ended, with the result that many projects in progress had to be suspended and some factories and mines which were conducting trial production could not go into production according to schedule.

The Moscow Conference (November 1960)

A commission of representatives of 26 Communist parties met in Moscow in September to prepare a draft policy statement for the forthcoming conference. According to Chinese sources, the Soviet delegation agreed to important changes in the draft which it had submitted, but withdrew its consent after Mr. Khrushchev returned on Oct. 14 from New York, where he had been attending the U.N. General Assembly. The Soviet party issued on Nov. 5 its reply to the Chinese letter of Sept. 10, which strongly criticized Mao Tse-tung and the Chinese party leadership.

The conference opened on Nov. 11, and was attended by representatives of 81 Communist parties; the Yugoslav League of Communists was not invited. Although it took place in conditions of strict secrecy, many details of the proceedings have since become known from material published by a number of the parties taking part.

The Chinese position was stated on Nov. 14 by **Teng Hsiao-ping,** who protested against the Soviet letter of Nov. 5 and maintained that it misrepresented the Chinese viewpoint. He denied that the Chinese party considered a world war inevitable, although it regarded one as probable while capitalism existed. Reaffirming that "just" local wars must be supported and counter-revolutionary local wars resisted, he pointed out that such local wars as the Suez campaign of 1956 had not led to world war. The Chinese party wanted world peace, but this could not be built on the goodwill of imperialist politicians, and talk of total disarmament was dishonest and misleading.

In colonial countries, he continued, the workers and peasants must ally themselves with the bourgeoisie in the struggle against imperialism, but after independence a struggle against the bourgeoisie was inevitable. In India, he alleged, the Government was manufacturing frontier incidents in order to postpone its own overthrow, but instead of supporting China in this situation the U.S.S.R. had taken the Indian Government's side. After accusing the Soviet party of over-estimating the possibility of a peaceful transition to Socialism and defending the Chinese party's economic policy, Teng dealt in conclusion with the question of relations between Communist parties. Although the Soviet party was the "leading party," he said, there were no "superior" or "inferior" parties; all Communist parties were independent and equal, and the Soviet party therefore could not claim to bind others by the resolutions passed by its congresses.

Teng was strongly supported by **Mr. Enver Hoxha,** leader of the Albanian Party of Labour, who alleged that at the Bucharest Conference the Soviet leaders had tried to rush through a condemnation of the Chinese party, and that they had exercised "unbearable pressures" to force Albania to join a bloc against China; when in August, as a result of floods and drought, Albania had had only 15 days' supply of wheat in stock, the U.S.S.R. had promised after 45 days' delay to supply 10,000 tons, or 15 days' supply, instead of the 50,000 needed, with delivery to be spread over two months. The only other parties which consistently supported the Chinese, however, were the Burmese, Malayan, and Australian parties.

30

The conference concluded on Nov. 25, and a 20,000-word statement summarizing its conclusions was published on Dec. 5. In general it represented a victory for Soviet views, although in the wording some concessions were made to the Chinese viewpoint. Its main points were as follows (cross-headings inserted):

War and Peace. "The aggressive nature of imperialism has not changed," the statement said, "but real forces have appeared that are capable of foiling its plans of aggression. War is not fatally inevitable . . . World war can be prevented by the joint efforts of the world Socialist camp, the international working class, the national liberation movement, all the countries opposing war, and all peace-loving forces . . . The policy of peaceful co-existence is also favoured by a definite section of the bourgeoisie of the developed capitalist countries, which takes a sober view of the relationship of forces and of the dire consequences of a modern war . . . But should the imperialist maniacs start war, the peoples will sweep capitalism out of existence and bury it . . .

"The near future will bring the forces of peace and Socialism new successes. The U.S.S.R. will become the leading industrial Power of the world. China will become a mighty industrial State. The Socialist system will be turning out more than half the world industrial product. The peace zone will expand . . . In these conditions a real possibility will have arisen of excluding world war from the life of society even before Socialism achieves complete victory on earth, with capitalism still existing in a part of the world . . .

"Peaceful co-existence of countries with different social systems does not mean conciliation of the Socialist and bourgeois ideologies. On the contrary, it implies intensification of the struggle of the working class, of all the Communist parties, for the triumph of Socialist ideas. But ideological and political disputes between States must not be settled through war . . ."

Colonial and Under-developed Countries. "Communists have always recognized the progressive, revolutionary significance of national liberation wars," the statement continued. "The peoples of the colonial countries win their independence both through armed struggle and by non-military methods, depending on the specific conditions in the country concerned . . .

"The urgent tasks of national rebirth facing the countries that have shaken off the colonial yoke cannot be effectively accomplished unless a determined struggle is waged against imperialism and the remnants of feudalism by all the patriotic forces of the nation, united in a single national democratic front . . . The alliance of the working class and the peasantry is the most important force in winning and defending national independence, accomplishing far-reaching democratic transformations, and ensuring social progress . . . The extent to which the national bourgeoisie participates in the liberation struggle depends to no small degree upon its strength and stability . . . In present conditions the national bourgeoisie of the colonial and dependent countries unconnected with imperialist circles is objectively interested in the accomplishment of the principal tasks of the anti-imperialist, anti-feudal revolution, and therefore retains the capacity of participating in the revolutionary struggle against imperialism and feudalism. In that sense it is progressive. But it is unstable, and is inclined to compromise with imperialism and feudalism . . .

"After winning political independence the peoples seek solutions to the

31

social problems raised by life and to the problems of reinforcing national independence. Different classes and parties offer different solutions. Which course of development to choose is the internal affair of the peoples themselves. As social contradictions grow, the national bourgeoisie inclines more and more to compromise with domestic reaction and imperialism. The people, however, begin to see that the best way to abolish age-long backwardness and improve their living standard is that of non-capitalist development . . . The Communist parties are working actively for a consistent completion of the anti-imperialist, anti-feudal democratic revolution . . . They support those actions of national Governments leading to the consolidation of the gains achieved and undermining the imperialists' positions. At the same time they firmly oppose anti-democratic, anti-popular acts and those measures of the ruling circles which endanger national independence . . ."

Forms of Transition to Socialism. The statement repeated verbatim the section of the 1957 declaration dealing with the possibility of a peaceful transition to Socialism.

Revisionism and Dogmatism. After condemning "the personality cult, which shackles creative thought and initiative," the statement repeated the 1957 declaration's formula that "revisionism . . . remains the main danger," but that "dogmatism and sectarianism . . . can also become the main danger at some stage of development of individual parties." In conclusion, it referred to the Soviet party as "the universally recognized vanguard of the world Communist movement," and described the decisions of its 20th congress as initiating "a new stage in the world Communist movement."

Soviet and Chinese Relations with Albania and Yugoslavia (1961)

After the Moscow Conference both the U.S.S.R. and China temporarily refrained from public polemics, and the signing of agreements on economic, scientific, and technical co-operation on June 19, 1961, of which no details were given, suggested that the U.S.S.R. was prepared to resume economic aid to China. The continued difference in their positions, however, was made clear by their contrasting attitudes towards Albania and Yugoslavia. The signing of agreements providing for increased trade between China and Albania and a Chinese loan to Albania were announced on Feb. 3, 1961, in a communiqué which emphasized the two Governments' complete agreement on ideological questions. Relations between the U.S.S.R. and Albania, on the other hand, deteriorated in 1961, and eight Soviet submarines which had been stationed at a base off the Albanian coast were withdrawn in May. Whereas the Chinese Press continued its violent attacks on "the Tito clique," Soviet relations with Yugoslavia showed a steady improvement during the same period; a five-year trade agreement was signed in March, and Mr. Popovich (the Yugoslav Foreign Minister) visited Moscow in July.

The 22nd Soviet Party Congress (October 1961)

The 22nd congress of the Soviet Communist Party, held on Oct. 17–31, widened the breach between the U.S.S.R. and China. Stalin and the "personality cult" were strongly criticized by Mr. Khrushchev and other speakers, and it was decided to remove his body from the Lenin Mausoleum. The congress also adopted a new party programme, which stated *inter alia* that "the dictatorship of the proletariat has fulfilled its historic mission, and has ceased to be indispensable to the U.S.S.R. from the point of view of the tasks of internal development . . . The dictatorship of the proletariat will cease to be necessary before the State withers away. The State as an organization embracing the entire population will survive until the final victory of Communism . . . As a result of the victory of Socialism in the U.S.S.R. and the consolidation of the unity of Soviet society, the Communist Party of the working class has become the vanguard of the Soviet people, a party of the entire people." These formulations were strongly criticized in later Chinese statements.

The congress resulted in an open break between the U.S.S.R. and Albania. In his report Mr. Khrushchev said on Oct. 17 that the Albanian leaders "have begun to depart from the common agreed line of the Communist movement of the whole world on major issues . . . They are themselves using the same methods as were current in our country at the time of the personality cult." Chou En-lai, addressing the congress on Oct. 19, commented that "if a dispute or differences unfortunately arise between fraternal parties or fraternal countries, they should be patiently resolved in the spirit of proletarian internationalism and on the principles of equality and unanimity, through consultation. Any public, one-sided censure of any fraternal party does not help unity, nor is it helpful in resolving problems. To lay bare a dispute between fraternal parties or fraternal countries, openly in the face of the enemy, cannot be regarded as a serious Marxist-Leninist attitude." This statement was welcomed on the following day by the central committee of the Albanian Party of Labour, which accused Mr. Khrushchev of "anti-Marxist lies."

Chou En-lai left for Peking on Oct. 23, without waiting for the end of the congress.

In a speech on Oct. 27 Mr. Khrushchev accused the Albanian leaders of "bloody atrocities," and declared that "all that was bad in our country at the time of the personality cult manifests itself in even worse form in the Albanian Party of Labour." On Chou En-lai's speech he commented. "We share the anxiety expressed by our Chinese friends, and appreciate their concern for greater unity. If the Chinese comrades wish to make efforts towards normalizing the relations between the Albanian Party of Labour and the fraternal parties, there is hardly anyone who could contribute more to the solution of this problem."

Diplomatic relations between the U.S.S.R and Albania were broken off in December. The Chinese party, while nominally remaining neutral, made obvious its support for Albania; the *People's Daily*, for example, gave great praise in November to Mr. Hoxha's "correct leadership" and "uncompromising struggle against modern revisionists."

Proposals for New International Conference (February–April 1962)

Proposals for a new international Communist conference were put forward at the beginning of 1962 by the Communist parties of Indonesia, North Vietnam, Great Britain, Sweden, and New Zealand. The central committee of the Soviet party expressed its support for this proposal in a letter to the Chinese party on Feb. 22, and suggested that "public statements liable to sharpen and not to smooth out our differences be given up." The Chinese party's reply (April 7) proposed as preliminary steps towards such a conference the ending of public attacks; bilateral or multilateral talks between parties; and the restoration of normal relations between the Soviet and Albanian Governments and Communist parties, with the U.S.S.R. taking the initiative. Although no further steps were taken at the time, a virtual truce from public polemics was in fact observed throughout the spring and summer.

IV: THE CONFLICT INTENSIFIES, 1962–64

Three events in the autumn of 1962—the re-establishment of friendly relations between the U.S.S.R. and Yugoslavia, the Cuban crisis, and the Sino-Indian War—led to a renewal of polemics, in which both sides soon abandoned the pretence that their attacks were directed against Yugoslavia or against Albania.

The Soviet-Yugoslav Rapprochement (May–October 1962)

During a visit to Bulgaria Mr. Khrushchev said in a speech at Varna on May 16, 1962, that the U.S.S.R. must do everything to co-operate with Yugoslavia and thus help her to consolidate her Socialist position, following which anti-Yugoslav polemics disappeared from the Soviet Press. Mr. Brezhnev, then the Soviet Head of State, paid an official visit to Yugoslavia from Sept. 24 to Oct. 4, at the beginning of which he said that Soviet policy towards Yugoslavia was based on the principles laid down in Mr. Khrushchev's Varna speech.

In China Mr. Brezhnev's visit provoked an intensification of anti-Yugoslav propaganda, and on Sept. 28 the Communist Party's central committee issued a statement violently attacking "the Tito clique," which, it declared, had "become still more despicable in betraying the cause of Communism and meeting the needs of imperialism." At this session of the committee Mao Tse-tung, who since 1958 had played a subordinate role in the leadership to Liu Shao-chi, Teng Hsiao-ping and Chou En-lai, began his struggle to regain supreme power—a process which was accompanied by an intensification of the ideological conflict with the U.S.S.R., and culminated in the Cultural Revolution of 1966–68.

The Cuban Crisis (October 1962)

President Kennedy stated on Oct. 22 that the U.S. Government had unmistakable evidence of the installation in Cuba of Soviet missile sites capable of delivering nuclear warheads to large areas of the U.S.A. and Central America, and that "a strict quarantine on all offensive military equipment under shipment to Cuba" would be imposed until the missile bases had been removed under U.N. supervision. The crisis ended when President Kennedy gave an assurance on Oct. 27 that the U.S.A. would not invade Cuba, and in return Mr. Khrushchev agreed on the following day to the dismantling of the Soviet bases. The Chinese Government showed its disapproval of this compromise by organizing mass anti-American demonstrations; a telegram sent to the Cuban Government on Oct. 29 by a demonstration in Peking declared that "650,000,000 Chinese will always remain the most faithful and reliable comrades-in-arms of the Cuban people and stand by them through thick and thin."

Soviet Military Aid to India—The Sino-Indian War (October–November 1962)

An agreement for the delivery of Soviet *Mig* fighters for the Indian Air Force and the building of a factory under licence in India to make these aircraft was concluded in the summer of 1962. Although the first *Migs* did not reach India until Feb. 11, 1963, after the Sino-Indian War, the agreement caused great offence in China, in view of her strained relations with India.

36

Fighting between the Chinese and Indian forces broke out on Oct. 20, 1962, both on India's north-east frontier and in Ladakh. In the North-East Frontier Agency the Chinese advanced over 100 miles south, threatening the plains of Assam, but in Ladakh they did not advance beyond the line claimed as Chinese territory. On Nov. 21 the Chinese announced a unilateral cease-fire and the withdrawal of their troops.

The Soviet Government adopted a reserved attitude towards the crisis, expressing overt support for neither side. *Pravda* called on Nov. 5 for a cease-fire and immediate talks between India and China "without any conditions attached."

Communist Party Congresses (November–December 1962)

The deepening of the crisis inside the world Communist movement was illustrated by developments at the Bulgarian, Hungarian, Italian, and Czechoslovak Communist Party congresses, which took place in November and December. At the Bulgarian congress, held on Nov. 5–14, Mr. Todor Zhivkov (the party's first secretary) denounced the Albanian leaders in terms which were clearly intended to apply to the Chinese also.

"The Albanian leaders," he said, "stop at nothing. They invent the vilest lies and spread them all over the world . . . They have proclaimed nearly all the fraternal Marxist-Leninist parties as being bogged down by 'contemporary' or 'modern' revisionism. To keep silent about the sectarian and adventurist actions of the Albanian leaders and their hypocritical splitting activities has never been and cannot be a serious Marxist-Leninist attitude"— the last phrase being a deliberate quotation from Chou En-lai's speech at the 22nd Soviet party congress.

Disputes between the Chinese delegation and those from the European parties occurred at the congress of the Hungarian Socialist Workers' Party, held on Nov. 20–24, but Mr. Kadar (the party's first secretary) adopted a conciliatory attitude, appealing to the Chinese delegation to take into account the views expressed at the congress, just as, he assured them, the Hungarian party would take note of the Chinese position. At the Italian party congress, however, held on Dec. 2–8, the dispute was at last brought into the open, when Signor Pajetta (a member of the party's Secretariat) directly criticized the Chinese position and commented that "a party like ours does not need to say Albania when it means China."

Signor Togliatti (the party's general secretary) emphasized that a nuclear war would mean the destruction of civilization; defended Soviet policy during the Cuban crisis as having safeguarded Cuban independence; condemned the conflict between China and India as "irrational and absurd"; and deplored the Albanians' "campaign of calumnies and insults" and the Chinese party's "unacceptable solidarity" with them. He also warned the Chinese delegation that "when you say capitalism has been restored in Yugoslavia—and everybody knows that is not true—nobody believes the rest of what you say."

The same issues were openly debated at the Czechoslovak party congress, held on Dec. 4–8. The Chinese delegation submitted a letter to the congress proposing "an international consultation of all Communist parties" to discuss the differences between them.

Mr. Khrushchev's Foreign Policy Speech (December 1962)

In a speech to the Supreme Soviet on Dec. 12 Mr. Khrushchev defended his policy during the Cuban crisis; commented on the Sino-Indian conflict and relations with Albania and Yugoslavia; and implied that Albanian attacks on the U.S.S.R. had been instigated by China.

"During the peaceful adjustment of the conflict in the Caribbean," he said, "shrill voices of discontent could be heard from people who call themselves Marxist-Leninists, even though their actions have nothing in common with Marxism-Leninism. I mean specifically the Albanian leaders. Their criticism of the Soviet Union in effect echoed that coming from the most reactionary, bellicose circles of the West. Why is it that the loudest shouts today come precisely from the Albanian leaders? I should like to recount an incident from my life to explain this. . . .

"I remember that in mining settlements foul-mouthed people sometimes used to find a small boy who had barely begun to articulate words without yet understanding what they meant and teach him the most foul language. They would tell him: 'Go to that house and say this to the people there.' Sometimes they did even worse. 'Go to your mother,' they would say, 'and repeat these words to her. Here are three kopecks for you. Afterwards we'll give you five.' And the child would run to the window, or to his mother, and repeat the foul words. . . . The Albanian leaders are like those unreasoning boys. Someone has taught them foul language, and they go about and use it against the Soviet Communist Party. And yet it is their mother! And for using this foul language they get the promised three kopecks. And if they use stronger and cruder language they get another five kopecks. . . ."

On the Sino-Indian conflict he said: "For the first time a situation has arisen in which a serious armed clash has resulted from a frontier dispute between a Socialist country and a country which has started on the road of independent development and is pursuing a policy of non-alignment. . . .

"We regard as reasonable the steps taken by the Government of China when it announced that it had unilaterally ceased fire and started to withdraw its troops. We are most happy about that, and welcome such actions on the part of the Chinese comrades.

"Some might say: 'How is it that you claim this is a reasonable step, if it was taken after so many lives had been lost and after so much blood had been shed? Would it not have been better if both sides had refrained from resorting to arms?' Yes, of course that would have been better. . . . But if it was not possible to prevent such a course of events, it is better to display courage now and to end the clash. . . .

"But there are some people who try to put a different interpretation on the decision taken by the Government of China. They ask: 'Isn't this a retreat?' They also ask: 'Isn't this a concession on the part of the Chinese comrades?' Of course, such questions are asked by those who love to cavil."

Commenting on the rapprochement with Yugoslavia, Mr. Khrushchev said: "Some people contend that Yugoslavia is not a Socialist country. It is then permissible to ask: what sort of a country is it? . . . There have been no landlords or capitalists in Yugoslavia for a long time now, and no private capital, no private enterprises or private estates, no private banks. . . . Therefore . . . it is impossible to deny that Yugoslavia is a Socialist country. And it is from this that we proceed in our policy, on this that we base our relations with Yugoslavia. . . ."

Mr. Khrushchev referred to the 1960 Moscow Conference's statement, and remarked: "The conference of fraternal parties warned that, unless a consistent struggle was waged against sectarianism and dogmatism, they might become the main danger at some particular stage in the development of individual parties. Events which have since taken place in the Communist movement show how far-sighted that conclusion was.

"Some people . . . place a lop-sided emphasis only on the danger from revisionism, mentioning Yugoslav revisionism in and out of context. But one must take a concrete view of things. In the crisis over Cuba, the Yugoslav Communists took a correct stand, while the dogmatists who pose as true Marxist-Leninists took a provocative one. . . . The crisis over Cuba showed specifically that it was those who took and are taking their stand on dogmatic positions who presented the main danger. . . ."

Chinese Replies to Foreign Criticism
(December 1962–January 1963)

The *People's Daily* replied to Mr. Khrushchev's speech on Dec. 15, and to Signor Togliatti on Dec. 31.

Defending Mao Tse-tung's slogan "imperialism is only a paper tiger," which Mr. Khrushchev had ridiculed in his speech, the *People's Daily* of Dec. 15 maintained that Communists should "despise the enemy on the strategic level while taking him seriously on the tactical level." Accusing Mr. Khrushchev of "defeatism" and "adventurism," it said: "If you dare not make the enemy feel your strength and contempt, that is defeatism. But if you pursue rash tactics, you fall irredeemably into adventurism. By acting in this way without daring to use your strength, you commit both mistakes at once. . . . We neither requested the introduction of offensive weapons into Cuba nor obstructed their withdrawal. No one can reproach us with adventurism, still less with plunging the whole world into a nuclear war."

The article went on to accuse "those who criticize us" over the Sino-Indian hostilities of being more sympathetic to the "Indian reactionaries" than to the Chinese Communists. Denouncing the use of party congresses as a platform for attacking other Communist parties, it said that this "monstrous practice" had originated at the Soviet party's 1961 congress—the only direct reference to the U.S.S.R. in the article. In conclusion, it repeated the proposal for an international Communist conference.

The *People's Daily* repeated many of these arguments on Dec. 31 in another long article entitled *The Differences between Comrade Togliatti and Us*. This maintained that the Chinese party's views on the question of war were those expressed in the 1960 Moscow statement, and accused Signor Togliatti of "bourgeois pacifism." On the Cuban crisis it commented: "We have never considered it a Marxist-Leninist attitude to brandish nuclear weapons as a way of settling international disputes. Nor have we ever considered that the avoidance of nuclear war in the Caribbean crisis was a 'Munich.' What we did strongly oppose . . . is the sacrifice of another country's sovereignty as a means of reaching a compromise with imperialism." Asserting that "the extent to which Comrade Togliatti and other comrades [an obvious reference to Mr. Khrushchev] have departed from Marxism-Leninism . . . is clearly revealed by their ardent flirtation with the Yugoslav revisionist group," the *People's Daily* contended that the condemnation of Yugoslav policy contained in the Moscow statement was still binding on all Communist parties.

The Soviet leadership gave its fullest exposition of its case to date in a 10,000-word article published in *Pravda* on January 7, 1963.

Pravda defended Soviet foreign policy along similar lines to Mr. Khrushchev's speech of Dec. 12, and again condemned the description of imperialism as a "paper tiger," on the ground that "such phrases can only sow complacency among the people and blunt their vigilance." Maintaining that the Soviet party still supported the Moscow statement, it commented that "some people lay a one-sided emphasis on the struggle against revisionism only, and at times decry creative Marxism-Leninism as revisionism." It went on to accuse the Albanian leaders "and those who support them" of themselves departing from the letter and spirit of the Moscow statement by launching "an unceremonious attack on the unity of the Communist movement," whereas the *rapprochement* between the Soviet Union and Yugoslavia was intended to promote such unity.

"The steps taken recently by the Yugoslav Communists and their leaders in their home and foreign policy have removed much of what was erroneous and damaging to the cause of building Socialism in Yugoslavia," the article continued. "Those who allege that 'capitalism has been restored in Yugoslavia' . . . lie deliberately. . . . The Soviet Communist Party openly declares that there still exist differences with the League of Communists of Yugoslavia on a number of ideological questions. But the *rapprochement* between Yugoslavia and the country building Communism can undoubtedly help in overcoming the differences on a number of ideological questions much quicker. . . ."

The *People's Daily*, replying on Jan. 27, quoted earlier attacks on Yugoslavia by Mr. Khrushchev, and commented that "we cannot understand why some comrades who formerly took a correct stand on Yugoslav revisionism have now made an about turn of 180 degrees."

Soviet Proposal for Talks accepted by Chinese Party (January–May 1963)

At the congress of the East German Socialist Unity Party, held on Jan. 15–21, Mr. Khrushchev defended the Soviet viewpoint without directly mentioning China. He called for "a halt to polemics between Communist parties," and opposed the holding of an immediate international conference on the ground that it would lead to the danger of a split. The Chinese delegate, Wu Hsiu-chuan, welcomed the proposal for ending polemics but supported the holding of a conference at an early date. His speech was several times drowned by booing, whereas the Yugoslav delegate was loudly applauded.

On Feb. 21 the central committee of the Soviet party, in a letter to the Chinese party, expressed concern that "open, ever-sharpening polemics are shaking the unity of fraternal parties," and suggested a meeting between representatives of the two parties in preparation for an international conference. Before replying the Chinese party intensified its polemics against its opponents.

The *People's Daily* on Feb. 26 criticized the Soviet party's 20th congress, declaring that it had "both positive and negative aspects." The differences inside the international movement, it stated, had been brought into the open in September 1959 by the Camp David talks and the Tass statement on the Indian border dispute, when "for the first time in history a Socialist country condemned a fraternal Socialist country instead of condemning the armed provocations of the reactionaries of a capitalist country." "Certain comrades" had attacked the Chinese party for "its general line of Socialist construction, its Great Leap Forward, and its people's communes, and spread the slander that the Chinese party was carrying out an adventurist policy." After the Bucharest Conference "some comrades" had applied "economic and political pressure against China, perfidiously and unilaterally tearing up hundreds of agreements and contracts with a fraternal country."

Despite China's attempts at conciliation (the *People's Daily* went on) the

Soviet Union had ceased its economic aid to Albania and interfered in Albania's internal affairs. An "unprincipled compromise" had been reached on the Cuban question, and "a fraternal Socialist country" had "not only supported politically the anti-Chinese policy of the Nehru Government but supplied it with military aid." The climax of the attacks on the Chinese party had been reached at the East German congress, which had created "a serious danger of a split." Necessary pre-conditions for an international conference, it concluded, would be the ending of attacks on the Chinese and Albanian parties, and condemnation of the Yugoslavs as "traitors to the Communist cause."

A 100,000-word article entitled *More on the Differences between Comrade Togliatti and Us*, published in instalments in the *People's Daily* from Feb. 28 to March 3, taunted the Soviet leaders with being afraid to publish Chinese articles in the Soviet Press and with jamming Peking broadcasts. It accused Signor Togliatti of "revisionism" and "bourgeois Socialism," and in particular of rejecting revolution and the dictatorship of the proletariat in favour of parliamentary methods.

The central committee of the Chinese party, replying to the Soviet letter on March 9, repeated the proposals put forward in its letter of April 7, 1962, and said that it would suspend polemics, while reserving the right to reply to public attacks. The Soviet party replied on March 30, suggesting that talks might take place in Moscow in May.

The Soviet letter, which was conciliatory in tone, condemned "the splitting activities of the Albanian leaders" but said that the Soviet party had offered in February to enter into discussions with them, and was still prepared to do so. On Yugoslavia it stated: "We maintain . . . that it is a Socialist country, and in our relations with it we strive to establish closer relations between Yugoslavia and the Socialist commonwealth, in accordance with the policy pursued by the fraternal parties for the cementing together of all the anti-imperialist forces of the world. We also take into consideration the definite positive tendencies shown of late in Yugoslavia's economic and socio-political life. Meanwhile the C.P.S.U. is aware of the serious differences that exist with the League of Communists of Yugoslavia on several ideological questions, and considers it necessary to tell the Yugoslav comrades so frankly." Appealing for an end to polemics, the letter said: "We could have found much to say in defence of the Leninist policy of the C.P.S.U., in defence of the common line of the international Communist movement, in reply to groundless attacks made in articles recently carried by the Chinese Press. If we are not doing it now, it is only because we do not want to gladden the foes of the Communist movement. . . ."

It was agreed on May 9 that talks should open in Moscow on July 5.

The Chinese Party's "25 Points" (June 1963)

The central committee of the Chinese party approved on June 14 a 60,000-word reply to the Soviet letter of March 30, which was delivered in Moscow on the following day and immediately published in the *People's Daily*. This letter, which put forward 25 points for discussion at the Moscow talks, was the fullest statement of the Chinese case yet issued. Although it nowhere mentioned Mr. Khrushchev, directing its criticisms against "certain persons" without giving names, it contained a comprehensive indictment of his policy and theoretical statements since 1956.

The 25 points set out in the Chinese letter are summarized below.

(1) "For several years there have been differences within the international Communist movement. . . . The central issue is . . . whether or not to accept the fact that the people still living under the imperialist and capitalist system . . . need to make revolution, and whether or not to accept the fact that the people already on the Socialist road . . . need to carry their revolution forward to the end. . . .

(2) "The revolutionary principles of the 1957 declaration and the 1960 statement [see pages 12 and 31] . . . may be summarized as follows: . . . Workers of the world, unite with the oppressed peoples; . . . bring the proletarian world revolution step by step to complete victory; and establish a new world without imperialism, without capitalism, and without the exploitation of man by man. . . .

(3) "If the general line of the international Communist movement is one-sidedly reduced to 'peaceful coexistence,' 'peaceful competition,' and 'peaceful transition,' this is to violate the revolutionary principles of the 1957 declaration and the 1960 statement. . . .

(4) "The fundamental contradictions in the contemporary world . . . are: the contradiction between the Socialist camp and the imperialist camp; the contradiction between the proletariat and the bourgeoisie in the capitalist countries; the contradiction between the oppressed nations and imperialism; and the contradictions among imperialist countries and among monopoly capitalist groups. . . .

(5) "The following erroneous views should be repudiated . . . : (a) the view which blots out the class content of the contradiction between the Socialist and imperialist camps . . . ; (b) the view which recognizes only the contradiction between the Socialist and imperialist camps . . . ; (c) the view which maintains . . . that the contradiction between the proletariat and the bourgeoisie can be resolved without a proletarian revolution in each country and that the contradiction between the oppressed nations and imperialism can be resolved without revolution . . . ; (d) the view which denies that the development of the inherent contradictions in the contemporary capitalist world inevitably leads to a new situation in which the imperialist countries are

43

locked in an intense struggle, and asserts that the contradictions among the imperialist countries can be reconciled or even eliminated by 'international agreements among the big monopolies'; and (e) the view which maintains that the contradiction between the two world systems of Socialism and capitalism will automatically disappear in the course of 'economic competition,' . . . and that a 'world without wars,' a new world of 'all-round cooperation,' will appear. . . .

(6) "Now that there is a Socialist camp consisting of 13 countries—Albania, Bulgaria, China, Cuba, Czechoslovakia, the German Democratic Republic, Hungary, the Democratic People's Republic of Korea, Mongolia, Poland, Romania, the Soviet Union, and the Democratic Republic of Vietnam— . . . the touchstone of proletarian internationalism is whether or not it resolutely defends the whole of the Socialist camp. . . ." [The formula "a Socialist camp of 13 countries," including Albania and Cuba but not Yugoslavia, had only recently come into use; the *People's Daily* in December 1961 had referred to the "12 fraternal countries," Cuba not being regarded as Socialist at that time.]

"If anybody . . . does not defend the unity of the Socialist camp but on the contrary creates tension and splits within it, or even follows the policies of the Yugoslav revisionists, tries to liquidate the Socialist camp, or helps capitalist countries to attack fraternal Socialist countries, he is betraying the interests of the entire international proletariat. . . ." [This passage was obviously directed against the Soviet Union and particularly against Soviet military aid to India.]

"If anybody, following in the footsteps of others, defends the erroneous opportunist line and policies pursued by a certain Socialist country instead of upholding the correct Marxist-Leninist line . . . he is departing from Marxism-Leninism and proletarian internationalism.

(7) "The 1960 statement points out: . . . 'U.S. imperialism is the main force of aggression and war.' . . . To make no distinction between enemies, friends, and ourselves, and to entrust the fate of the people and of mankind to collaboration with U.S. imperialism, is to lead people astray. . . .

(8) "Certain persons in the international Communist movement are now taking a passive or scornful or negative attitude towards the struggles of the oppressed nations for liberation. . . . The attitude taken towards the revolutionary struggles of the people in the Asian, African, and Latin American countries is an important criterion for differentiating those who want revolution from those who do not. . . .

(9) "The oppressed nations and peoples of Asia, Africa, and Latin America are faced with the urgent task of fighting imperialism and its lackeys. . . . In these areas extremely broad sections of the population refuse to be slaves of imperialism. They include not only the workers, peasants, intellectuals, and petty bourgeoisie, but also the patriotic national bourgeoisie and even certain kings, princes, and aristocrats. . . . The proletariat and its party must . . . organize a broad united front against imperialism. . . . The proletarian party should maintain its ideological, political, and organizational independence and insist on the leadership of the revolution. The proletarian party and the revolutionary people must learn to master all forms of struggle, including armed struggle. . . . The policy of the proletarian party should be . . . to unite with the bourgeoisie, in so far as they tend to be progressive, anti-imperialist, and

anti-feudal, but to struggle against their reactionary tendencies to compromise and collaborate with imperialism and the forces of feudalism. . . .

(10) "In the imperialist and capitalist countries the proletarian revolution and the dictatorship of the proletariat are essential. . . . It is wrong to refuse to use parliamentary and other legal forms of struggle when they can and should be used. However, if a Marxist-Leninist party falls into legalism or parliamentary cretinism, confining the struggle within the limits permitted by the bourgeoisie, this will inevitably lead to renouncing the proletarian revolution and the dictatorship of the proletariat.

(11) "Marx and Lenin did raise the possibility that revolutions may develop peacefully. But, as Lenin pointed out, the peaceful development of revolution is an opportunity 'very seldom to be met with in the history of revolution.' As a matter of fact, there is no historical precedent for peaceful transition from capitalism to Socialism. . . . The proletarian party must never base its thinking, its policies for revolution, and its entire work on the assumption that the imperialists and reactionaries will accept peaceful transformation. . . .

(12) "If the leading group in any party adopt a non-revolutionary line and convert it into a reformist party, then Marxist-Leninists inside and outside the party will replace them and lead the people in making revolution. . . . There are certain persons who assert that they have made the greatest creative contributions to revolutionary theory since Lenin and that they alone are correct. But it is very dubious . . . whether they really have a general line for the international Communist movement which conforms with Marxism-Leninism. . . .

(13) "Certain persons have one-sidedly exaggerated the role of peaceful competition between Socialist and imperialist countries in their attempt to substitute peaceful competition for the revolutionary struggles of the oppressed peoples. According to their preaching, it would seem that imperialism will automatically collapse in the course of this peaceful competition, and that the only thing the oppressed peoples have to do is to wait quietly for the advent of this day. What does this have in common with Marxist-Leninist views?

"Moreover, certain persons have concocted the strange tale that China and some other Socialist countries want to 'unleash wars' and to spread Socialism by 'wars between States.' As the statement of 1960 points out, such tales are nothing but imperialist and reactionary slanders. To put it bluntly, the purpose of those who repeat these slanders is to hide the fact that they are opposed to revolutions by the oppressed peoples and nations of the world and opposed to others supporting such revolutions.

(14) "Certain persons say that revolutions are entirely possible without war. . . . If they are referring to a war of national liberation or a revolutionary civil war, then this formulation is, in effect, opposed to revolutionary wars and to revolution. If they are referring to a world war, then they are shooting at a non-existent target. Although Marxist-Leninists have pointed out, on the basis of the history of the two World Wars, that world wars inevitably lead to revolution, no Marxist-Leninist ever has held or ever will hold that revolution must be made through world war.

"Marxist-Leninists take the abolition of war as their ideal and believe that war can be abolished. But how can war be abolished? . . . Certain persons now actually hold that it is possible to bring about 'a world without weapons,

45

without armed forces, and without wars' through 'general and complete disarmament' while the system of imperialism and of the exploitation of man by man still exists. This is sheer illusion. . . .

"If one regards general and complete disarmament as the fundamental road to world peace, spreads the illusion that imperialism will automatically lay down its arms, and tries to liquidate the revolutionary struggles of the oppressed peoples and nations on the pretext of disarmament, then this is deliberately to deceive the people of the world and help the imperialists in their policies of aggression and war. . . . World peace can be won only by the struggles of the people in all countries and not by begging the imperialists for it. . . .

(15) "The complete banning and destruction of nuclear weapons is an important task in the struggle to defend world peace. We must do our utmost to this end. . . . However, if the imperialists are forced to accept an agreement to ban nuclear weapons, it decidedly will not be because of their 'love for humanity,' but because of the pressure of the people of all countries and for the sake of their own vital interests. . . .

"The emergence of nuclear weapons does not and cannot resolve the fundamental contradictions in the contemporary world, does not and cannot alter the law of class struggle, and does not and cannot change the nature of imperialism and reaction. It cannot, therefore, be said that with the emergence of nuclear weapons the possibility and the necessity of social and national revolutions have disappeared, or that the basic principles of Marxism-Leninism, and especially the theories of proletarian revolution and the dictatorship of the proletariate . . . have become outmoded . . .

(16) "It was Lenin who advanced the thesis that it is possible for the Socialist countries to practise peaceful co-existence with the capitalist countries. . . . The People's Republic of China, too, has consistently pursued the policy of peaceful co-existence with countries having different social systems, and it is China which initiated the Five Principles of Peaceful Co-existence.

"However, a few years ago certain persons suddenly claimed Lenin's policy of peaceful co-existence as their own 'great discovery.' They maintain that they have a monopoly in the interpretation of this policy. They treat 'peaceful co-existence' as if it were an all-inclusive, mystical book from heaven, and attribute to it every success the people of the world achieve by struggle. What is more, they label all who disagree with their distortions of Lenin's views as opponents of peaceful co-existence. . . .

"Lenin's principle of peaceful co-existence . . . designates a relationship between countries with different social systems. . . . It should never be extended to apply to the relations between oppressed and oppressor nations, between oppressed and oppressor countries, or between oppressed and oppressor classes, and never be described as the main content of the transition from capitalism to Socialism. Still less should it be asserted that peaceful co-existence is mankind's road to Socialism. . . .

"The general line of the foreign policy of the Socialist countries should have the following content: to develop relations of friendship, mutual assistance, and co-operation among the countries of the Socialist camp in accordance with the principle of proletarian internationalism; to strive for peaceful co-existence on the basis of the Five Principles with countries having different social systems, and oppose the imperialist policies of aggression and war; and to support and assist the revolutionary struggles of all the oppressed peoples and

46

nations. These three aspects are inter-related and indivisible, and not a single one can be omitted.

(17) "For a very long historical period after the proletariat takes power, class struggle continues. . . . To deny the existence of class struggle in the period of the dictatorship of the proletariat and the necessity of thoroughly completing the Socialist revolution on the economic, political, and ideological fronts . . . violates Marxism-Leninism.

(18) "The fundamental thesis of Marx and Lenin is that the dictatorship of the proletariat will inevitably continue for the entire historical period of the transition from capitalism to Communism. . . . If it is announced, half-way through, that the dictatorship of the proletariat is no longer necessary . . . this would lead to extremely grave consequences and make any transition to Communism out of the question. . . .

"Is it possible to replace the State of the dictatorship of the proletariat by a 'State of the whole people'? This is not a question of the internal affairs of any particular country, but a fundamental problem involving the universal truth of Marxism-Leninism. . . . In calling a Socialist State the 'State of the whole people,' is one trying to replace the Marxist-Leninist theory of the State by the bourgeois theory of the State? Is one trying to replace the State of the dictatorship of the proletariat by a State of a different character? . . .

(19) "Is it possible to replace the party which is the vanguard of the proletariat by a 'party of the entire people'? This, too, is not a question of the internal affairs of any particular party, but a fundamental problem involving the universal truth of Marxism-Leninism. . . . What will happen if it is announced half-way before entering the higher stage of Communist society that the party of the proletariat has become a 'party of the entire people' and if its proletarian class character is repudiated? . . . Does this not disarm the proletariat and all the working people, organizationally and ideologically, and is it not tantamount to helping to restore capitalism? . . .

(20) "Over the past few years certain persons have violated Lenin's integral teachings about the inter-relationship of leaders, party, class, and masses, and raised the issue of 'combating the personality cult'; that is erroneous and harmful. . . . To raise the question of 'combating the personality cult' is actually to counterpose the leaders to the masses, undermine the party's unified leadership, which is based on democratic centralism, dissipate its fighting strength, and disintegrate its ranks. . . .

"While loudly combating the so-called personality cult, certain persons are in reality doing their best to defame the proletarian party and the dictatorship of the proletariat. At the same time, they are enormously exaggerating the role of certain individuals, shifting all errors on to others, and claiming all credit for themselves. What is more serious is that, under the pretext of 'combating the personality cult,' certain persons are crudely interfering in the internal affairs of other fraternal parties and fraternal countries, and forcing other fraternal parties to change their leadership in order to impose their own wrong line on these parties. What is this if not great-Power chauvinism, sectarianism, and splittism? . . .

(21) "Relations between Socialist countries, whether large or small, and whether more developed or less developed economically, must be based on the principles of complete equality. . . . Every Socialist country must rely mainly on itself for its construction. . . . If, proceeding only from its own partial interests, any Socialist country unilaterally demands that other fraternal coun-

47

tries submit to its needs, and uses the pretext of opposing what they call 'going it alone' and 'nationalism' to prevent other fraternal countries from applying the principle of relying mainly on their own efforts in their construction and from developing their economies on the basis of independence, or even goes to the length of putting economic pressure on other fraternal countries— then these are pure manifestations of national egoism. . . . In relations among Socialist countries it would be preposterous to follow the practice of gaining profit for oneself at the expense of others . . . or go so far as to take the 'economic integration' and the 'Common Market,' which monopoly capitalist groups have instituted for the purpose of seizing markets and grabbing profits, as examples which Socialist countries ought to follow in their economic co-operation and mutual assistance."

[This section apparently referred to differences which had arisen between the Soviet Union and Romania at a Comecon meeting in February, when the Romanian delegate objected to proposals for co-ordination of economic plans which would have involved cuts in Romania's industrial development programme.]

(22) "If the principle of independence and equality is accepted in relations among fraternal parties, then it is impermissible for any party to place itself above others, to interfere in their internal affairs, and to adopt patriarchal ways in relations with them. If it is accepted that there are no 'superiors' and 'subordinates' in relations among fraternal parties, then it is impermissible to impose the programme, resolutions, and line of one's own party on other fraternal parties as the 'common programme' of the international Communist movement.

"If the principle of reaching unanimity through consultation is accepted in relations between fraternal parties, then one should not emphasize 'who is in the majority' or 'who is in the minority,' and bank on a so-called majority in order to force through one's own erroneous line and carry out sectarian and splitting policies. If it is agreed that differences between fraternal parties should be settled through inter-party consultation, then other fraternal parties should not be attacked publicly and by name at one's own party congress or other party congresses, in speeches by party leaders, resolutions, statements, etc.; and still less should the ideological differences among fraternal parties be extended into the sphere of State relations. . . .

"In the sphere of relations among fraternal parties and countries, the question of Soviet-Albanian relations is an outstanding one at present. . . . How to treat the Marxist-Leninist fraternal Albanian Party of Labour is one question. How to treat the Yugoslav revisionist clique of traitors to Marxism-Leninism is quite another question. These two essentially different questions must on no account be placed on a par.

"Your letter says that you 'do not relinquish the hope that the relations between the C.P.S.U. and the Albanian Party of Labour may be improved,' but at the same time you continue to attack the Albanian comrades for what you call 'splitting activities." Clearly this is self-contradictory and in no way contributes to resolving the problem of Soviet-Albanian relations.

"Who is it that has taken splitting actions in Soviet-Albanian relations? Who is it that has extended the ideological differences between the Soviet and Albanian parties to State relations? Who is it that has brought the divergences between the Soviet and Albanian parties and between the two countries into the open before the enemy? Who is it that has openly called for a change in the Albanian party and State leadership? All this is plain and clear to the whole world. . . . We once again express our sincere hope that the leading comrades of the C.P.S.U. will observe the principles guiding relations among fraternal parties and countries and take the initiative in seeking an effective way to improve Soviet-Albanian relations. . . .

"The comrades of the C.P.S.U. state in their letter that 'the Communist Party of the Soviet Union has never taken and will never take a single step that could show hostility among the peoples of our country toward the fraternal Chinese people or other peoples.' Here we do not desire to enumerate the many unpleasant events that have occurred in the past; we only wish that the comrades of the C.P.S.U. will strictly abide by this statement in their future actions. During the past few years our party members and our people have exercised the greatest restraint in the face of a series of grave incidents which were in violation of the principles guiding relations among fraternal parties and countries. . . . The spirit of proletarian internationalism of the Chinese Communists and the Chinese people has stood a severe test. . . .

(23) "Certain persons are now attempting to introduce the Yugoslav revisionist clique into the Socialist community and the international Communist ranks. This is openly to tear up the agreement unanimously reached at the 1960 meeting of the fraternal parties and is absolutely impermissible.

"Over the past few years . . . the many experiences and lessons of the international Communist movement have fully confirmed the correctness of the conclusion in the [Moscow] declaration and the statement that revisionism is at present the main danger in the international Communist movement. However, certain persons are openly saying that dogmatism and not revisionism is the main danger, or that dogmatism is no less dangerous than revisionism. . . . Genuine Marxist-Leninist parties . . . must not barter away principles, approving one thing today and another tomorrow. . . .

"It is necessary at all times to adhere to the universal truth of Marxism-Leninism. Failure to do so will lead to right opportunist or revisionist errors. On the other hand, it is always necessary to proceed from reality . . . and independently work out and apply policies and tactics suited to the conditions of one's own country. Errors of dogmatism will be committed if one fails to do so, if one mechanically copies the policies and tactics of another Communist Party, submits blindly to the will of others, or accepts without analysis the programme and resolutions of another Communist Party as one's own line. Some people are now violating this basic principle. . . . On the pretext of 'creatively developing Marxism-Leninism' they cast aside the universal truth of Marxism-Leninism. Moreover, they describe as 'universal Marxist-Leninist truths' their own prescriptions, which are based on nothing but subjective conjecture . . . , and they force others to accept these prescriptions unconditionally. That is why so many grave phenomena have come to pass in the international Communist movement. . . .

(24) "If a party is not a proletarian revolutionary party but a bourgeois reformist party; if it is not a Marxist-Leninist party but a revisionist party; . . . if it is not a party that can use its brains to think for itself . . . but instead is a party that parrots the words of others, copies foreign experience without analysis, runs hither and thither in response to the baton of certain persons abroad, and has become a hodgepodge of revisionism, dogmatism, and everything but Marxist-Leninist principle; then such a party is absolutely incapable of leading the proletariat and the masses in revolutionary struggle. . . .

(25) "The public polemics in the international Communist movement have been provoked by certain fraternal party leaders and forced on us. Since a public debate has been provoked, it ought to be conducted on the basis of equality among fraternal parties . . . and by presenting the facts and reasoning things out. . . . Since certain party leaders have published innumerable articles attacking other fraternal parties, why do they not publish in their own Press the articles those parties have written in reply?

"Latterly, the Communist Party of China has been subjected to preposterous attacks. . . . We have published these articles and speeches attacking us in our own Press. . . . Between Dec. 15, 1962, and March 8, 1963, we wrote seven articles in reply to our attackers. . . . Presumably you are referring to these articles when towards the end of your letter of March 30 you accuse the Chinese Press of making 'groundless attacks' on the C.P.S.U. It is turning things upside down to describe articles replying to our attackers as 'attacks.'

"Since you describe our articles as 'groundless' and as so very bad, why do you not publish all seven of these 'groundless attacks' in the same way as we have published your articles, and let all the Soviet comrades and Soviet people think for themselves and judge who is right and who wrong? You are of course entitled to make a point-by-point refutation of these articles you consider 'groundless attacks.' Although you call our articles 'groundless' and our arguments wrong, you do not tell the Soviet people what our arguments actually are. This practice can hardly be described as showing a serious attitude towards the discussion of problems by fraternal parties, towards the truth, or towards the masses. . . ."

The letter ended by saying that "there are other questions of common concern, such as the criticism of Stalin and some important matters of principle regarding the international Communist movement which were raised at the 20th and 22nd congresses of the C.P.S.U., and we hope that on these questions, too, there will be a frank exchange of opinion in the [Moscow] talks."

Chinese Embassy Officials Expelled from U.S.S.R. (June 1963)

The central committee of the Soviet party, a plenary session of which opened on June 18, announced on the same day that the Chinese letter would not be published in the Soviet Union "at the present time," as its "unwarranted attacks" on the Soviet and other Communist parties would call for "a public reply which would lead to a further sharpening of polemics." A communiqué issued by the committee on June 21, rejected the Chinese attacks on the Soviet party, on the decisions of its 20th, 21st, and 22nd congresses, and on its programme as "groundless and slanderous."

The Soviet Government demanded on June 27 the recall of three Chinese Embassy officials who had distributed copies of the Chinese letter in the U.S.S.R., this demand being described by the Chinese Foreign Ministry as "unreasonable and unfriendly." A Soviet Foreign Ministry statement of July 4 said that members of the Chinese Embassy staff had disseminated a specially printed mass edition of the letter in the Russian language in Moscow and other cities, despite two protests from the Soviet Foreign Ministry. A Chinese Note protesting against the expulsions, published on July 5, maintained that "it is perfectly normal for the official organs and personnel of one Socialist country in another Socialist country to distribute the published documents of their own Government and party."

The Moscow Talks (July 1963)

Talks between the two parties began in Moscow on July 5 under conditions of strict secrecy, the Chinese party being represented by Teng Hsiao-ping, Peng Chen, and Wu Hsiu-chuan, and the Soviet party by Mr. Suslov, Mr. Andropov, Mr. Ponomarev, Mr. Ilyichev, and Mr. Chervonenko (the Soviet Ambassador in Peking). They ended on July 20 without agreement being reached; a communiqué issued on the following day said that at the Chinese delegation's suggestion it had been decided "to have an interval in the work of the delegations and to continue the meeting some time later, at a place and time to be agreed upon."

The Soviet Reply to the "25 Points" (July 1963)

The Chinese letter of June 14 was published in *Pravda* on July 14, together with an 18,000-word reply which took the form of an open letter from the Soviet central committee to the party membership. This accused the Chinese leaders of being prepared to sacrifice hundreds of millions of lives in a nuclear war, of advocating the revival of Stalin's methods of government, and of organizing disruptive activities inside other Communist parties, and suggested that they were inspired by nationalist and racialist rather than by Communist principles. The Soviet letter is summarized below (crossheadings inserted):

Introduction. "The frankly hostile actions of the C.P.C. leaders, their persistent striving to sharpen polemics in the international Communist movement, the deliberate distortion of the positions of our party, and the incorrect

51

interpretation of the motives for which we refrained temporarily from publishing the letter," it said, "impel us to publish the letter of the C.P.C. central committee of June 14, 1963, and to give our appraisal of this document. All who read the letter of the C.P.C. central committee will see, behind the bombastic phrases about unity and cohesion, unfriendly and slanderous attacks on our party and our country. . . .

"The document is crammed with charges—overt and covert—against the C.P.S.U. and the Soviet Union. The authors of the letter permit themselves unworthy fabrications, insulting to Communists, about 'the betrayal of the interests of the whole international proletariat and all the peoples of the world' and 'a departure from Marxism-Leninism and proletarian internationalism.' They hint at 'cowardice in face of the imperialists,' at 'a step back in the course of historic development,' and even at 'the organizational and moral disarming of the proletariat and all working people,' which is tantamount to 'helping to restore capitalism' in our country. . . ."

Soviet Aid to China. Commenting that the Chinese leaders had "recently sought to belittle the significance of Soviet aid," the letter recalled that the Soviet Union had helped China to build 198 industrial enterprises and other projects, and to establish such new branches of industry as automobile, tractor, and aircraft manufacturing; had supplied China with over 1,400 blueprints of big enterprises; had trained thousands of specialists and workers; and was still providing technical assistance in the construction of 88 enterprises.

Development of the Controversy. The letter stated that at the 1960 Moscow Conference, when the majority of Communist parties rejected the C.P.C.'s views, the Chinese delegation had "stubbornly upheld its own particular views, and signed the statement only when the danger arose of its complete isolation." Shortly afterwards they had resumed their propaganda, "using the leadership of the Albanian Party of Labour as a mouthpiece." A series of subsequent appeals aimed at improving relations had found no response in Peking.

The Chinese leaders, the letter claimed, had carried their ideological differences into international relations by curtailing their economic and trade relations with the U.S.S.R. and other Socialist countries. "On the initiative of the Chinese Government, the volume of China's trade with the Soviet Union has been cut almost 67 per cent in the past three years, and deliveries of industrial plant have dropped to one-fortieth."

From the end of 1961 the Chinese representatives in international organizations had begun openly to demand the exclusion of Soviet delegates and those of other European Communist countries from conferences in Africa or Asia.

War and Peace. "At a first glance," the Soviet letter commented, "many theses in the [Chinese] letter may seem puzzling. Whom are the Chinese comrades actually arguing with? Are there Communists who, for instance, object to Socialist revolution or who do not regard it as their duty to fight against imperialism and to support the national liberation movement? . . . The Chinese comrades first ascribe to the C.P.S.U. and other Marxist-Leninist parties views which they have never expressed and which are alien to them; secondly, by paying lip-service to formulae and positions borrowed from the documents of the Communist movement, they try to camouflage their erroneous views. . . .

"In point of fact, however, the questions which bear on vital interests of the peoples are in the centre of the dispute. These are the questions of war and peace, the role and development of the world Socialist system, the struggle against the ideology and practice of the personality cult, the strategy and tactics of the world labour movement, and the national liberation struggle. . . .

"The world Communist movement, in the declaration and statement, set before Communists as a task of extreme importance that of struggling for peace and averting a nuclear world catastrophe. . . . Though the nature of imperialism has not changed and the danger of the outbreak of war has not been averted, in modern conditions the forces of peace, of which the mighty community of Socialist States is the main bulwark, can by their joint efforts avert a new world war. . . .

"The nuclear rocket weapons which have been created . . . possess an unprecedented devastating force. . . . Have Communists the right to ignore this danger? Must we tell the people the whole truth about the consequences of nuclear war? We believe that, without question, we must. This cannot have a 'paralyzing' effect on the masses, as the Chinese comrades assert. On the contrary, the truth about modern war will mobilize the will and energy of the masses in the struggle for peace and against imperialism. . . .

"What is the position of the C.P.C. leadership? What do the theses that they propagate mean—that an end cannot be put to war so long as imperialism exists? That peaceful co-existence is an illusion? That it is not the general line of the foreign policy of Socialist countries? That the peace struggle hinders the revolutionary struggle? . . . They do not believe in the possibility of pre-venting a new world war; they underestimate the forces of peace and Socialism and overestimate the forces of imperialism; in fact, they ignore the mobilization of the masses for the struggle against the war danger. . . .

Nuclear War. "The Chinese comrades obviously underestimate the whole danger of nuclear war," the letter continued. " 'The atomic bomb is a paper tiger, it is not terrible at all,' they contend. The main thing is to put an end to imperialism as quickly as possible, but how and with what losses this will be achieved seems to be a secondary question. To whom, it is right to ask, is it secondary? To the hundreds of millions of people who are doomed to death in the event of the unleashing of a nuclear war? To the States that will be erased from the face of the earth in the very first hours of such a war? . . .

"Some responsible Chinese leaders have also declared that it is possible to sacrifice hundreds of millions of people in war." [This referred to a statement made by Mao Tse-tung at the 1957 Moscow conference.] " 'On the ruins of destroyed imperialism,' asserts *Long Live Leninism*, which was approved by the C.P.C. central committee, 'the victorious peoples will create with tremendous speed a civilization a thousand times higher than the capitalist system, and will build their bright future.' Is it permissible to ask the Chinese comrades if they realize what sort of ruins a nuclear world war would leave behind? . . . They say frankly, 'On the ruins of a destroyed imperialism'— in other words, as a result of the unleashing of war—'a bright future will be built.' If we agree to this, then indeed there is no need for the principle of peaceful co-existence. . . .

"We ourselves produce the nuclear weapon and have manufactured it in sufficient quantity. We know its destructive force full well. If imperialism starts a war against us we shall not hesitate to use this formidable weapon against the aggressor; but if we are not attacked, we shall not be the first to use this weapon. . . .

53

"We would like to ask the Chinese comrades who suggest building a 'bright future' on the ruins of the old world destroyed by a nuclear war whether they have consulted the working class of the countries where imperialism dominates . . . The nuclear bomb does not distinguish between the imperialists and working people. . . .

"The posing of the question in this way by the Chinese comrades may give rise to the well-justified suspicion that this is no longer a class approach in the struggle for the abolition of capitalism, but has entirely different aims. If both the exploiters and the exploited are buried under the ruins of the old world, who will build the 'bright future'? In this connexion it is impossible not to note the fact that instead of the internationalist class approach expressed in the call 'Workers of the world, unite,' the Chinese comrades propagate the slogan, which is devoid of any class meaning, 'The wind from the east prevails over the wind from the west.' . . ."

The Cuban Crisis. The letter went on: "The Chinese comrades allege that in the period of the Caribbean crisis we made an 'adventurist' mistake by introducing rockets into Cuba and then 'capitulated' to American imperialism when we removed the rockets from Cuba. Such assertions utterly contradict the facts. What was the actual state of affairs? The C.P.S.U. central committee and the Soviet Government possessed trustworthy information that an armed aggression by U.S. imperialism against Cuba was about to take place. . . . Proceeding from the need to defend the Cuban revolution, the Soviet Government and the Cuban Government reached agreement on the delivery of missiles to Cuba. . . . Such a resolute step on the part of the Soviet Union and Cuba was a shock to the American imperialists, who felt for the first time in their history that if they were to undertake an armed invasion of Cuba, a shattering retaliatory blow would be dealt against their own territory.

"Inasmuch as the point in question was not simply a conflict between the United States and Cuba, but a clash between the two major nuclear Powers, the crisis in the Caribbean area would have turned from a local into a world one. A real danger of nuclear war arose. There was one alternative in the prevailing situation: either to . . . embark upon a course of unleashing a world nuclear war, or, profiting from the opportunity offered by the delivery of missiles, to take all steps to reach an agreement on a peaceful solution of the crisis and to prevent aggression against Cuba. As is known, we chose the second path. . . . Agreement to remove the missile weapons in return for the U.S. Government's commitment not to invade Cuba . . . made it possible to frustrate the plans of the extreme adventurist circles of American imperialism. . . .

"The Chinese comrades regard our statement that the Kennedy Government also displayed a certain reasonableness and a realistic approach in the Cuban crisis as 'prettifying imperialism.' Do they really think that all bourgeois Governments lack all reason in everything they do? . . . The Chinese comrades argue that the imperialists cannot be trusted in anything, that they are bound to cheat. But this is not a case of good faith, but rather one of sober calculation. Eight months have passed since the elimination of the Caribbean crisis, and the U.S. Government is keeping its word—there has been no invasion of Cuba. We also assumed a commitment to remove our missiles from Cuba, and we have fulfilled it. It should not, however, be forgotten that we have given a commitment to the Cuban people: if the U.S. imperialists do not keep their promise but invade Cuba, we shall come to the assistance of the Cuban people. . . .

"What are the Chinese leaders dissatisfied with? Is it perhaps the fact that it was possible to prevent the invasion of Cuba and the unleashing of a world war? . . .

Disarmament. "The true position of the C.P.C. leadership is demonstrated very clearly . . . in its complete underestimation and, what is more, deliberate ignoring of the struggle for disarmament," the Soviet letter went on. "They try to prove that general disarmament is possible only when Socialism triumphs all over the world. Must the Marxists sit on their hands, waiting for the victory of Socialism all over the world, while mankind suffocates in the clutches of the arms race? . . . One can repeat *ad infinitum* that war is inevitable, claiming that such a viewpoint is evidence of one's 'revolutionary spirit.' In fact, this approach merely indicates lack of faith in one's strength and fear of imperialism. . . .

Peaceful Co-existence. "The C.P.C. central committee accuses the Communist parties of extending peaceful co-existence between States with different social systems to relations between the exploiters and the exploited, between the oppressed and the oppressing classes, between the working masses and the imperialists. This is a truly monstrous fabrication. . . . When we speak of peaceful co-existence we mean the inter-State relations of the Socialist countries with the countries of capitalism. The principle of peaceful co-existence, naturally, can in no way be applied to relations between the antagonistic classes inside the capitalist States. . . .

The Personality Cult and the Dictatorship of the Proletariat. "The C.P.C. leaders have taken on themselves the role of defenders of the personality cult, of propagators of Stalin's wrong ideas. They are trying to thrust upon other parties the practices, ideology, ethics, and forms and methods of leadership which flourished in the period of the personality cult." The letter went on to quote statements made in 1956 by Mao Tse-tung, Liu Shao-chi, and Teng Ksiao-ping fully supporting the decisions of the 20th congress of the C.P.S.U., including its condemnation of the "personality cult," and commented that "they have made a turn of 180 degrees in evaluating the 20th congress of our party."

Describing the results of "the restoration of Leninist principles and standards in party life," the letter said: "The atmosphere of fear, suspicion, and uncertainty which poisoned the life of the people in the period of the personality cult has gone. . . . Ask the people whose fathers and mothers were victims of the reprisals in the period of the personality cult what it means for them to obtain recognition that their fathers, mothers, and brothers were honest people, and that they themselves are not outcasts in our society. . . .

"Soviet people find it strange and outrageous that the Chinese comrades should be trying to smear the C.P.S.U. programme," the letter continued. "Alluding to the fact that our party proclaims as its task the struggle for a better life for the people, the C.P.C. leaders hint at some sort of 'bourgeoisification' and 'degeneration' of Soviet society. To follow their line of thinking, it seems that if a people walks in rope sandals and eats watery soup out of a common bowl, that is Communism, and if a working man lives well and wants to live even better tomorrow, that is almost tantamount to the restoration of capitalism! . . .

Methods of Revolutionary Struggle. "The next important question on which we differ is that of ways and methods of the revolutionary struggle of the working class. As depicted by the Chinese comrades, the differences on this question appear as follows: one side—they themselves—stands for world revolution, while the other—the C.P.S.U., the Marxist-Leninist parties—have forgotten the revolution and even fear it, and instead of revolutionary struggle are concerned with things unworthy of a real revolutionary, such as peace, the economic development of the Socialist countries, the improvement of the living standards of their peoples, and the struggle for the democratic rights and vital interests of the working people of the capitalist countries. . . .

"Lenin taught that 'we exert our main influence on the international revolution by our economic policy' . . . But now it turns out that there are comrades who have decided that Lenin was wrong. What is this—lack of faith in the ability of the Socialist countries to defeat capitalism in economic competition? Or is it the attitude of persons who, on meeting with difficulties in building Socialism, have become disappointed and do not see the possibility of exerting the main influence on the international revolutionary movement by their economic successes? . . . They want to achieve the revolution sooner, by other and what seem to them shorter ways. But the victorious revolution can consolidate its successes and prove the superiority of Socialism over capitalism by the work, and only by the work of the people. . . .

"The Chinese comrades, in a haughty and abusive way, accuse the Communist parties of France, Italy, the United States, and other countries of nothing less than opportunism and reformism, of 'parliamentary cretinism,' even of slipping down to 'bourgeois Socialism.' On what grounds do they do this? On the grounds that these Communist parties do not put forward the slogan of an immediate proletarian revolution, although even the Chinese leaders must realize that this cannot be done without the existence of a revolutionary situation. . . .

"The Chinese comrades have also disagreed with the world Communist movement on the forms of the transition of different countries to Socialism. . . . The Chinese comrades regard as the main criterion of revolutionary spirit recognition of the armed uprising. . . . [They] are thereby in fact denying the possibility of using peaceful forms of struggle for the victory of the Socialist revolution, whereas Marxism-Leninism teaches that Communists must master all forms of revolutionary class struggle, both violent and non-violent.

National Liberation Movements. "Yet another important question is that of the relationship between the struggle of the international working class and the national liberation movement of the peoples of Asia, Africa, and Latin America," the letter continued. ". . . These are the great forces of our epoch. Correct co-ordination between them constitutes one of the main prerequisites for victory over imperialism.

"How do the Chinese comrades solve this problem? This is seen from their new theory, according to which the main contradiction of our time is not between Socialism and imperialism, but between the national liberation movement and imperialism. The decisive force in the struggle against imperialism, the Chinese comrades maintain, is not the world system of Socialism, not the struggle of the international working class, but the national liberation movement.

"In this way the Chinese comrades apparently want to win popularity among the peoples of Asia, Africa, and Latin America by the easiest possible means. But let no one be deceived by this theory. Whether the Chinese theoreticians want it or not, this theory in essence means isolating the national liberation movement from the international working class and its creation, the world system of Socialism. . . . The Chinese comrades . . . want to amend Lenin and prove that it is not the working class but the petty bourgeoisie or the national bourgeoisie, or even 'certain patriotically minded kings, princes, and aristocrats,' who must be the leaders of the world struggle against imperialism. . . .

"The question arises, what is the explanation for the incorrect propositions of the C.P.C. leadership on the basic problems of our time? It is either the complete divorcement of the Chinese comrades from actual reality—a dogmatic, bookish approach to problems of war, peace, and revolution; their lack of understanding of the concrete conditions of the present epoch—or the fact that behind the rumpus about the 'world revolution' raised by the Chinese comrades there are other goals, which have nothing in common with revolution. . . ."

Relations between Socialist Countries. Accusing the Chinese of "activities aimed at undermining the unity of the world Socialist camp and the international Communist movement," the letter stated that in the past three years China had reduced the volume of her trade with other Socialist countries by over 50 per cent, and by breaking its agreements had seriously harmed the economies of some of them. It went on: "The formula of 'building Socialism mainly by our own forces' [see point (21) of the Chinese letter] conceals the concept of creating self-sufficient national economies for which economic contacts with other countries are restricted to trade alone. The Chinese comrades are trying to impose this approach on other Socialist countries. . . . It cannot be regarded otherwise than as an attempt to undermine the unity of the Socialist commonwealth. . . ."

The International Communist Movement. The letter also accused the Chinese leadership of "organizing and supporting various anti-party groups of renegades," including dissident Communist groups in Belgium, the U.S.A., Brazil, Australia, Italy, India, and Ceylon; alleged that the Trotskyist Fourth International was trying to use the Chinese party's position to further its own ends; and said that the Chinese leaders had published in many languages abusive attacks on the Soviet, French, Italian, Indian, and U.S. Communist parties, and were "trying to subordinate other fraternal parties to their influence and control."

Albania and Yugoslavia. The letter stated that the Chinese leaders had done "everything in their power to use the Albanian leaders as their mouthpiece," and had "openly pushed them on to the road of open struggle against the Soviet Union."

Rejecting the Chinese view that Yugoslavia was not a Socialist country, the letter quoted a statement made by the *People's Daily* in 1955 that "Yugoslavia has achieved notable successes in the building of Socialism." The Soviet letter asked: "Why then have the Chinese leaders so drastically changed their attitude on the Yugoslav question? It is hard to find an explanation other than that they saw in this one of the pretexts advantageous, in their opinion, for discrediting the policy of the C.P.S.U. and other Marxist-Leninist parties.

"Differences on a number of ideological questions of principle continue to remain between the C.P.S.U. and the League of Communists of Yugoslavia," the letter continued. "But it would be wrong to 'excommunicate' Yugoslavia from Socialism on these grounds. . . . At the present time there are 14

Socialist countries in the world. . . . The range of questions encountered by the fraternal parties which stand at the helm of State is increasing, and besides this each of the fraternal parties is working in different conditions. It is not surprising that in these circumstances the fraternal parties may develop different approaches to the solution of this or that problem. . . .

"If we were to follow the example of the Chinese leaders, because of our serious differences with the leaders of the Albanian Party of Labour we should long since have proclaimed Albania to be a non-Socialist country. But that would be a wrong and subjective approach. In spite of our differences with the Albanian leaders, the Soviet Communists regard Albania as a Socialist country, and for their part do everything in their power to prevent Albania from being split away from the Socialist community. . . ."

Chinese Comments on Soviet Statement (July 1963)

The first public Chinese comment on the Soviet letter was made on July 19 by a spokesman of the C.P.C. central committee, who said that its contents "do not accord with the facts, and we cannot agree with the views it expresses."

The spokesman's statement, which was ironic in tone, announced that the Chinese central committee had decided to re-publish its letter of June 14 together with the Soviet reply, and also to broadcast both documents in many languages. "There is only one reason," he said, "why we are broadcasting the open letter of the central committee of the C.P.S.U.—it is a remarkable piece of work. To quote a Chinese poem:

A remarkable work should be enjoyed together
And doubts analysed in company."

He advised as many people as possible to study the Soviet letter, as it was "superlative material for learning by negative example."

The full text of the Soviet letter was published in the *People's Daily* on July 20, together with an editorial note which declared that "the methods used in the letter are the distortion of facts and the reversal of right and wrong—methods which Marxist-Leninists can in no circumstances tolerate."

The *People's Daily* accused the Soviet leaders of "trying to pin the vicious charge of bellicosity on China, and in particular to attack Comrade Mao Tse-tung."

In reply to the Soviet charge that the Chinese leaders had reversed their attitude towards the decisions of the 20th congress of the C.P.S.U., the *People's Daily* said that the Chinese party had never considered the 20th congress to be "wholly positive." It continued:

"We have never agreed with its complete negation of Stalin, an action it took on the pretext of combating the personality cult, or with its one-sided emphasis on peaceful transition. . . . We repeatedly pointed out that Stalin's merits outweighed his faults. . . . Similarly, on the question of peaceful transition, the central committee of the C.P.C. expressed differing opinions to the C.P.S.U. on many occasions. . . . At that time, however, we did not publicly criticize the leaders of the C.P.S.U., for the sake of safeguarding the solidarity of the international Communist movement and out of consideration for the prestige of the C.P.S.U. and the Soviet Union."

In reply to the Soviet allegation that China had extended ideological differences to the sphere of State relations, the *People's Daily* said that the withdrawal of Soviet experts in 1960 had "inflicted incalculable difficulties and losses on China's economy, national defence, and scientific research, and was the main reason for the reduction in the economic and commercial links between China and the Soviet Union. China is the victim. Yet the central committee of the C.P.S.U. in its open letter blames China for reducing economic and commercial links with the Soviet Union and for extending ideological differences to the sphere of State relations! So complete a reversal of the truth is indeed astonishing."

Chinese Denunciation of Nuclear Test-ban Treaty
(July 1963)

The Chinese Government issued a violently-worded statement on July 31 denouncing as a "dirty fraud" the partial nuclear test-ban treaty which had been initialled in Moscow on July 25 by the U.S.S.R., the U.S.A., and Britain. The statement said that the treaty "runs diametrically counter to the wishes of the peace-loving peoples," would not hinder America from pursuing her policy of "nuclear blackmail and proliferation of nuclear weapons," and represented an attempt on the part of America, Russia, and Britain to preserve their "nuclear monopoly." The exclusion of underground tests from the treaty's scope was regarded as particularly advantageous for "the further development of nuclear weapons by U.S. imperialism." The Soviet Government was accused of having "willingly allowed U.S. imperialism to get military superiority"; of having "betrayed the peoples of the Socialist camp," including the peoples of the U.S.S.R. and China; and of "allying with the forces of war and reaction against the forces of peace." Declaring that the peoples of the world wanted a real and not a "fake" peace, the Chinese statement said that the treaty reflected "the ugly face of U.S. imperialism, which is aggressive by nature, as well as the servile features of those who are warmly embracing American imperialism."

Chou En-lai sent identical letters on Aug. 2 to all Heads of State calling for a world conference of Heads of Government to discuss "the question of complete, thorough, total, and resolute prohibition of nuclear weapons." Apart from Albania, the only countries to accept this proposal were North Korea and North Vietnam, which at this time were sympathetic to China's views in the ideological controversy, and Pakistan, which in recent years had adopted a policy of close friendship with China.

Liu Shao-chi described the atomic bomb as a "paper tiger" in a speech on Sept. 18. Saying that "the decisive factor in war is man, not new types of weapons," he declared that "in the eyes of the modern revisionists to survive is everything. The philosophy of survival has replaced Marxism-Leninism."

The Soviet Government issued a lengthy statement on Aug. 3 in reply to the Chinese Government's statement of July 31. Describing the Chinese statement as "reeking of hopelessness and pessimism," the Soviet Government expressed amazement that any Socialist country could have issued such a declaration; replied sharply to the "impudent" allegations made by the Chinese Government; and described China's attitude as "tantamount to actual connivance with those who advocate thermo-nuclear world war and who are against the settlement round the conference table of international problems in dispute." The Chinese Government had thereby taken up a position which "runs counter to the Leninist policy of peaceful coexistence between States with different social systems," and the Chinese leaders had "placed themselves openly against the Socialist Commonwealth, the whole world Communist movement, and all the peace-loving peoples of Europe, Asia, Africa, and America."

A Soviet statement of Aug. 21 maintained that the real motive of the Chinese leaders' opposition to the treaty was their desire to acquire their own atomic bomb at any cost. In reply the Chinese Government accused the U.S.S.R. on Sept. 1 of giving the U.S.A. details of the secret agreement of 1957 on nuclear weapons.

Chinese Polemics against Soviet Party
(September 1963–February 1964)

A series of seven articles replying to the Soviet party's open letter of July 14 appeared between Sept. 6, 1963, and Feb. 10, 1964, in the *People's Daily* and *Red Flag*.

After an introductory article reviewing the history of the controversy, the next two articles respectively defended Stalin and attacked the Yugoslav regime as "a brutal Fascist dictatorship." The fourth described the Soviet leaders as "apologists for neo-colonialism" who adopted "a passive or scornful attitude" towards the struggles of the peoples of Asia, Africa, and Latin America, and accused them of inciting racial hatred by reviving the theory of the "yellow peril."

The fifth article, which dealt with the question of war and peace, said: "The leaders of the C.P.S.U. [Communist Party of the Soviet Union] hold that with the appearance of nuclear weapons there is no longer any difference between just and unjust wars, that oppressed peoples and nations must abandon revolution and refrain from waging just popular revolutionary wars and wars of national liberation, and that the Socialist countries must . . . yield to imperialist nuclear blackmail. . . . The C.P.C. [Communist Party of China] has always held that the Socialist countries should actively support the peoples' revolutionary struggles. . . . At the same time we hold that the oppressed peoples and nations can achieve liberation only by their resolute revolutionary struggle and that no one else can do it for them. . . . Socialist countries must not use nuclear weapons to support the peoples' wars of national liberation and revolutionary civil wars, and have no need to do so. . . . The Socialist countries must achieve and maintain nuclear superiority. Only this can prevent the imperialists from launching a nuclear war and help to bring about the complete prohibition of nuclear weapons. . . . In the hands of a Socialist country nuclear weapons must always be defensive weapons for resisting imperialist nuclear threats. A Socialist country must not be the first to use nuclear weapons, nor should it in any circumstances play with them or engage in nuclear blackmail and nuclear gambling"—as, the article maintained, Mr. Khrushchev had done during the Cuban crisis.

The sixth article accused Mr. Khrushchev of having turned the Marxist-Leninist concept of peaceful coexistence into a policy of "class capitulation," whilst the seventh denounced the Soviet leaders as "the greatest splitters of our times."

Polemics against the Chinese party's policy continued in the Soviet Press in the summer and autumn of 1963, but in general avoided personal vituperation of the type contained in the Chinese attacks on Mr. Khrushchev.

The C.P.S.U.'s theoretical organ *Kommunist* contended on Oct. 6, 1963, that although the C.P.C. now claimed to support peaceful coexistence, which it had formerly attacked, it did not rule out the possibility of an international "revolutionary war" begun by a Socialist State. "To strive to achieve revolution in other countries by means of world war," the article said, "is a path that is unacceptable to Communists in principle because it is based on the anti-Leninist idea of 'accelerating' revolution from outside. Moreover, it is a path which ignores the question of the real consequences of a world war fought by means of nuclear weapons. . . ."

On Oct. 23 *Kommunist* declared that Chinese propaganda was engaged in the "deification of Mao Tse-tung" and in "a campaign against the very fundamentals of Marxism-Leninism such as has not occurred since the days of Trotskyism." It was inspiring and supporting "anti-party and factional groups" in other countries, in an attempt to "knock together an international bloc out of such groups, mostly consisting of people who were expelled from Communist parties."

Soviet Proposals for World Communist Conference and Ending of Polemics (October 1963–February 1964)

During the autumn the Soviet Press published a large number of statements by foreign Communist parties calling for a world Communist conference in the near future. Mr. Khrushchev appealed on Oct. 25 for an end to public polemics, and suggested that if there were differences between the Chinese and Soviet parties "let us allow time to have its say as to which viewpoint is more correct." The New China News Agency, however, claimed on Nov. 15 that since this appeal Soviet papers had published more than 80 anti-Chinese articles, and described it as "nothing but a trick to cover up the Soviet leaders' frenzied anti-Chinese activities." On Nov. 29 the Soviet party, in a letter to the Chinese party, proposed a suspension of polemics in preparation for an international conference.

After emphasizing the harm done to the international Communist movement by public polemics, the letter observed that "besides the questions over which differences have arisen, there are also positions on which we are fully united or at least very close in our views." After appealing for "a calm and unprejudiced understanding of our present discussion and the elimination from it of everything that is non-essential," it proposed that negotiations should be opened on an increase of trade between the two countries and on increased Soviet technical aid to Chinese industry.

The letter suggested that public polemics should be replaced by an exchange of views through mutual consultations, negotiations, and exchanges of letters, which would create more favourable conditions for a world Communist conference. "It is the duty of all parties," it concluded, "to help to create a situation which will render such a meeting fruitful, so that it will lead not to a split in the world Communist movement but to the genuine unity and solidarity of all the fraternal parties. . . ."

The Soviet letter was ignored by the Chinese party, which did not reply until Feb. 29, 1964, and meanwhile continued to publish articles attacking the Soviet party and calling for the formation of pro-Chinese parties in countries where the local Communist leadership supported the U.S.S.R. The *People's Daily* on Feb. 4 openly advocated a split in the world Communist movement, maintaining that "like everything else, the international working-class movement tends to divide itself in two."

Mr. Suslov's Report to C.P.S.U. Central Committee (February 1964)

After the publication of this article, the Soviet leadership abandoned its conciliatory attitude. In an unpublished letter of Feb. 12, which was sent to other Communist parties but not to the Chinese party, they stated that the central committee would discuss the Chinese party's activities at its forthcoming plenary session and thereafter would openly state its views, and again raised the question of a world Communist conference. On Feb. 14 Mr. Suslov (a member of the party secretariat) presented a long report on the controversy to the central committee, containing the most comprehensive Soviet indictment of the Chinese leadership to date; the report, however, was not published at the time, at the Romanian party's request [see below].

Mr. Suslov accused the Chinese leaders of "steering a course towards a split among the Communist parties and towards the setting-up of factions and groups hostile to Marxism-Leninism," and of seeking "to give orders in the Socialist commonwealth as in their own estate, to impose their will on other countries, and to dictate the terms on which they would either admit parties and peoples into the Socialist system or 'excommunicate' them from it at will." As an example, he cited the Chinese attitude towards Yugoslavia, which they had praised in 1955–56 but now denounced as a "Fascist dictatorship."

Referring to the Albanian party, Mr. Suslov commented: "The Chinese-Albanian alliance . . . arose on the basis of opposition to the 20th congress of the C.P.S.U., on the basis of a hostile attitude to the elimination of the effects of the Stalin personality cult. Just as in the case of China, the defence by the Albanian leaders of the personality cult is due to the fact that for many years they have themselves been imposing the personality cult and using pernicious methods of leadership in the party and the country."

Mr. Suslov also accused the Chinese leaders of trying to sabotage the Soviet Union's efforts to avert the threat of a world war, as when in 1962 they had taken advantage of the Cuban crisis to extend the conflict on the Indian frontier. "The obviously adventurist position of the C.P.C. leaders makes itself seen in their attitude to the question of nuclear weapons," he went on. The Chinese leaders had sought insistently to obtain the nuclear bomb from the Soviet Union, and had expressed deep mortification when the U.S.S.R. did not give them samples of nuclear weapons. "We consider it inexpedient to help China to produce nuclear weapons," Mr. Suslov added. "The inevitable reaction to this would be the nuclear arming of Powers of the imperialist camp, in particular West Germany and Japan. Having a higher level of economic, scientific, and technical development, they could undoubtedly produce more bombs than China, and could build up a nuclear potential much faster."

Turning to the question of the transition from capitalism to Socialism, Mr. Suslov maintained that the Chinese leaders had rejected "the Leninist teaching that the Socialist revolution is the result of a mass struggle by the people" and were relying "solely on armed uprisings everywhere and in all cases, without taking into account the feelings of the masses of the people and their preparedness for revolution, or the internal and external situation." This approach rejected "painstaking and patient work with the masses and reliance on the maturing of the objective and subjective conditions for a Socialist revolution, in favour of revolutionary phrase-mongering, or, what is still worse, in favour of adventurist actions by a handful of men who are cut off from the people. . . ." Mr. Suslov commented: "If the Communist parties pin all their hopes solely on armed struggles, without taking into consideration the preparedness of the masses to support such a struggle, it will inevitably lead only to bitter failures."

After declaring that "the policy and activity of the Chinese leaders today are the main danger to the unity of the world Communist movement," Mr. Suslov continued: "Anti-party groups of renegades and splitters have been set up, with help and support from Peking, in Belgium, Brazil, Australia, Ceylon, Britain, and some other countries. Some of these groups number less than 10 members; others comprise a few dozen people. . . . The C.P.C. leadership is carrying things further, plainly intending to form in opposition to the world Communist movement a bloc of its fellow-thinkers which will have its own platform and group discipline, and will be centred on Peking. . . . The C.P.C. leadership is striving to spread the Mao Tse-tung personality cult to the whole world Communist movement, so that the leader of the C.P.C. may, like Stalin in his day, sit aloft like God above all the Marxist-Leninist parties and arbitrarily settle all questions of their policy and work. . . ."

The report concluded: "It is now perfectly clear that the C.P.C. leaders . . . intend to carry on with their factional activities in the world Communist movement. Our party favours convening another meeting of fraternal parties in order to discuss the basic problems of our time, and to hold the broadest possible exchange of opinions in the interest of surmounting the difficulties that have arisen in the Communist movement. These difficulties stem from the C.P.C. leadership's differences with the world Communist movement. A col-

64

lective effort by all the fraternal parties is therefore justified in order to deter-
mine the necessary ways and means for preserving and strengthening the
Marxist-Leninist unity of the Communist ranks. . . ."

Exchange of Correspondence between Chinese and Soviet Parties (February–March 1964)

The Soviet party's letter of Feb. 12 provoked a lengthy and
acrimonious correspondence between the Chinese and Soviet parties.

In a letter dated Feb. 20, the central committee of the Chinese party demanded to be sent a copy of the Soviet letter, and accused the Soviet leaders
of "vicious two-faced tactics," "posing as the 'father party,' " and intriguing for
"a sham unity and a real split." The Soviet reply (Feb. 22) pointed out that
the Chinese party had not yet replied to the Soviet letter of Nov. 29, and commented that "as you persistently failed to reply to our repeated letters and
approaches and, what is more, presented them as expressions of our weakness,
it was unnecessary and indeed useless to send you our letter of Feb. 12." A
second Chinese letter (Feb. 27) peremptorily repeated the demand to be sent
the letter of Feb. 12.

On Feb. 29 the central committee of the Chinese party replied at
length to the Soviet letter of Nov. 29; it expressed its willingness to
reach a negotiated settlement on the boundary question, but rejected
the offer of economic aid and put forward its own terms for the
holding of a world Communist conference. (The sub-headings below
are taken from the original.)

Economic Aid. "So far from being gratis," the letter declared, "Soviet aid to
China was rendered mainly in the form of trade and was certainly not a one-
way affair. China has paid and is paying the Soviet Union in goods, gold, or
convertible foreign exchange for all Soviet-supplied sets of equipment and
other goods, including those made available on credit plus interest. It is necessary to add that the prices of many of the goods we imported from the Soviet
Union were much higher than those on the world market.

"While China has received aid from the Soviet Union, the Soviet Union has
also received corresponding aid from China. . . . Up to the end of 1962
China furnished the Soviet Union with 2,100,000,000 new roubles' worth of
grain, edible oils, and other foodstuffs. . . . Over the same period, China furnished the Soviet Union with more than 1,400,000,000 new roubles' worth
of mineral products and metals. . . . Many of these mineral products are
raw materials indispensable for the development of the most advanced branches
of science and for the manufacture of rockets and nuclear weapons.

"As for the Soviet loans to China, it must be pointed out that China used
them mostly for the purchase of war material from the Soviet Union, the
greater part of which was used up in the war to resist U.S. aggression and aid
Korea. . . . For many years we have been paying the principal and interest on

these Soviet loans, which account for a considerable part of our yearly exports to the Soviet Union. . . ."

Technical Aid. "When the leaders of the C.P.S.U. unilaterally decided to recall all the Soviet experts in China," the letter continued, "we solemnly affirmed our desire to have them continue their work. . . . But in spite of our objections you . . . withdrew the 1,390 Soviet experts working in China, tore up 343 contracts and supplementary contracts concerning experts, and scrapped 257 projects of scientific and technical co-operation, all within the short space of a month. . . . Many of our important designing and scientific research projects had to stop half way, some of the construction projects in progress had to be suspended, and some of the factories and mines which were conducting trial production could not go into production according to schedule. . . . Now you have again suggested sending experts to China. To be frank, the Chinese people cannot trust you. . . ." The letter added ironically: "We are very much concerned about the present economic situation in the Soviet Union. If you should feel the need for the help of Chinese experts in certain fields, we would be glad to send them."

Sino-Soviet Trade. "Nobody is in a better position than you to know the real cause for the curtailment of Sino-Soviet trade over the last few years," the letter went on. "This curtailment was precisely the result of your extending the differences from the field of ideology to that of State relations. Your sudden withdrawal of all Soviet experts working in China upset the construction schedules and production arrangements of many of our factories, mines, and other enterprises, and had a direct impact on our need for the import of complete sets of equipment. Such being the case, did you expect us to keep on buying them just for display? . . .

"Since 1960 you have deliberately placed obstacles in the way of economic and trade negotiations between our two countries, and held up or refused supplies of important goods which China needs. You have insisted on providing large amounts of goods which we do not really need, or which we do not need at all, while holding back or supplying very few of the goods which we need badly. . . . From 1959 to 1961 our country suffered extraordinary natural disasters for three years in succession and could not supply you with as large quantities of agricultural produce and processed products as before. This was the result of factors beyond human control. . . .

"You constantly accuse us of 'going it alone,' and claim that you stand for extensive economic ties and division of labour among the Socialist countries. But what is your actual record in this respect? . . . You bully those fraternal countries whose economies are less advanced, oppose their policy of industrialization, and try to force them to remain agricultural countries for ever and serve as your sources of raw materials and as outlets for your goods. You bully fraternal countries which are industrially more developed, and insist that they stop manufacturing their traditional products and become accessory factories serving your industries. . . .

"We hold that it is necessary to transform the Council for Mutual Economic Assistance of Socialist countries (Comecon) to accord with the principle of proletarian internationalism, and to turn this organization—now solely controlled by the leaders of the C.P.S.U.—into one based on genuine equality and mutual benefit, which the fraternal countries of the Socialist camp may join of their own free will. It is hoped that you will favourably respond to our suggestion."

66

Public Polemics. The Chinese letter accused the C.P.S.U. of beginning public polemics with its attack on Albania at its 22nd congress in 1961 and continued: "What you did was a bad thing. You created difficulties for fraternal parties and rendered a service to the imperialists and reactionaries. Now, with the extensive unfolding of the public debate, the truth is becoming clearer and clearer and Marxism-Leninism is making more and more progress. What was a bad thing is becoming a good thing."

Between July 15, 1963, and the end of October, the letter maintained, the Soviet Press had published nearly 2,000 anti-Chinese articles and other items, and these had continued to appear even after the Soviet letter of Nov. 29. "We have so far printed only seven articles in reply to your open letter [of July 14, 1963]," it added. "We have not yet completed our reply to the important questions you raised in the open letter, and have not even started to reply to the questions you raised in your other anti-Chinese articles." The letter concluded with the following proposals:

(1) "For the cessation of public polemics it is necessary for the Chinese and Soviet parties and other fraternal parties to hold various bilateral and multilateral talks in order to find through consultation a fair and reasonable formula acceptable to all, and to conclude a common agreement.

(2) "The Chinese Communist Party consistently advocates and actively supports the convening of a meeting of representatives of all Communist and Workers' parties. . . . Together with the other fraternal parties, we will do everything possible to ensure that this meeting will be a meeting of unity on the basis of the revolutionary principles of Marxism-Leninism.

(3) "The resumption of talks between the Chinese and Soviet parties is a necessary preparatory step for making the meeting of the fraternal parties a success. We propose that the talks between the Chinese and Soviet parties be resumed in Peking from Oct. 10 to Oct. 25, 1964.

(4) "In order to make further preparations for the meeting of representatives of all fraternal parties, we propose that the Sino-Soviet talks be followed by a meeting of representatives of 17 fraternal parties—namely, the parties of Albania, Bulgaria, China, Cuba, Czechoslovakia, the German Democratic Republic, Hungary, Korea, Mongolia, Poland, Romania, the Soviet Union, and Vietnam, and the parties of Indonesia, Japan, Italy, and France."

In its reply to the Chinese letters of Feb. 27 and 29, 1964, the central committee of the Soviet party put forward on March 7 counter-proposals for a world Communist conference in the autumn.

The Soviet letter declared that "while deliberately delaying an official answer to our appeal [of Nov. 29], you in fact replied to it by inflaming polemics, by intensifying schismatic activities in the Communist movement, and by directing even more slanderous accusations at the C.P.S.U. and other Marxist-Leninist parties. . . . In these circumstances we could no longer remain silent. . . . There was no sense at all in sending you our letter addressed to other fraternal parties . . . if only because we had already repeatedly approached you with the same questions and received no answer. . . ."

Rejecting the Chinese charge that the C.P.S.U. was posing as the "father party," the letter commented: "We cannot avoid the impression that all this is done solely to enable you to fill the role of a 'father party' yourselves. But times are different now. Even in Stalin's lifetime this role had become obsolete, although he did take such a position. . . . Today the situation is not what it was, for instance, in 1919; today Lenin is no longer alive, and no one living can take his place. It is only collectively that the Marxist-Leninist parties can work out a common line for the Communist movement. There are no 'father' or 'son' parties, nor can there be any, but there is and must be a family of fraternal parties with equal rights and collective wisdom. . . ."

The Soviet letter did not attempt to reply to the charges contained in the Chinese letter of Feb. 29, concentrating on the question of a world conference. "We note," it stated, "that after many months of stalling and delay the C.P.C. has agreed with our view of continuing the bilateral meeting of representatives of the C.P.S.U. and the C.P.C., and of afterwards calling a meeting of all the Communist and Workers' parties. . . . At the same time, we do not understand your motives for delaying these measures for a long period. . . . The delaying of the bilateral meeting between representatives of the C.P.S.U. and the C.P.C. is all the more inexplicable. . . . Your proposal that the meeting . . . be held as late as October 1964 means in fact that the meeting of fraternal parties would be delayed by at least a year."

The letter rejected the Chinese proposal for a preparatory meeting of 17 parties, and suggested instead a meeting of representatives of the 26 parties which jointly prepared the 1960 Moscow statement—i.e., the 17 parties named in the Chinese letter, and in addition those of Western Germany, Britain, Finland, Argentina, Brazil, Syria, India, the United States, and Australia. It concluded with the following proposals: "(1) That the meeting of representatives of the C.P.S.U. and the C.P.C. be continued in Peking in May 1964. (2) That the preparatory meeting of representatives of 26 fraternal parties be called in June-July 1964. (3) That the international meeting be held, with the agreement of the fraternal parties, in the autumn of 1964."

In conclusion the Soviet letter declared: "The central committee of the C.P.S.U. emphasizes that for the successful implementation of all these measures it is necessary that there be a cessation of public polemics and an abandonment of all types of subversive and schismatic activity in the Socialist community and the Communist movement. . . ."

Unsuccessful Romanian Attempt at Mediation (February–March 1964)

The Romanian Workers' Party, which throughout the controversy had played an independent role, attempted in February and March to act as a mediator between the two sides. After receiving the Soviet letter of Feb. 12, the Romanian leadership appealed to the Soviet party not to publish Mr. Suslov's report, and to the Chinese party to put an immediate end to polemics, and suggested a meeting of the leadership of the two parties. The Soviet party agreed to delay publication of the report on condition that the Chinese ceased public polemics, whilst the Chinese party agreed to a temporary truce and invited a Romanian delegation to visit Peking.

Talks took place in Peking on March 2–11 between a Romanian delegation headed by the Prime Minister, Mr. Maurer, and a Chinese delegation headed by Liu Shao-chi, but produced little result, as the Chinese leaders maintained that polemics could be stopped only after an agreement on the conditions of their cessation had been reached through bilateral or multilateral discussions.

In a new attempt to avoid an open split, President Gheorghiu-Dej on March 25 handed to the Soviet and Chinese Ambassadors in Bucharest a draft appeal to all Communist parties for unity, and proposed that a joint commission of Soviet, Chinese, and Romanian party officials should make preparations for an international conference comprising "all Communist parties of the world, not merely certain parties." The Soviet party agreed to examine the Romanian proposals, but no reply was received from the Chinese party.

Renewal of Polemics (March–April 1964)

Both sides had abstained from public polemics while the Sino-Soviet correspondence and the Romanian attempt at mediation were in progress, but at the end of March the truce was broken by the Chinese. Their new propaganda offensive was launched at the sixth meeting of the Afro-Asian Solidarity Council, held in Algiers on March 22–26.

Members of the Chinese delegation accused the Soviet Government *inter alia* of "racialism," "imperialism," "betraying the Algerian revolution," "refusing to help the Arabs to liberate Palestine," and being "morally responsible for the murder of Patrice Lumumba" (the former Premier of the Congo murdered in 1961). The leader of the Soviet delegation retorted by accusing the Chinese of "trying to set countries and whole continents against one another, on the principle of 'divide and rule.'" Most of the other delegations refused to align themselves with either side.

The eighth and longest of the series of articles replying to the Soviet open letter was published in Peking on March 31.

The article was largely devoted to refuting Mr. Khrushchev's "gross error" that in certain conditions there could be a peaceful transition from capitalism to Socialism, and contended that "to realize the transition to Socialism the proletariat must wage armed struggle, smash the old State machine, and establish a dictatorship of the proletariat." Admitting that the 1957 declaration and the 1960 statement, both of which the Chinese party had signed, envisaged the possibility of either a peaceful or a non-peaceful transition, it

69

alleged that the Soviet draft had referred only to the peaceful variety, and that the non-peaceful one had been added only after a great deal of argument; the Chinese party, it added, was willing to accept criticism for agreeing to compromise on this issue. The rest of the article was largely devoted to personal invective against Mr. Khrushchev, who was described as having "assumed the mantle of Trotsky," as "the greatest capitulationist in history," and as leading the Soviet Union back to capitalism. The article advised "leading comrades" of the Soviet party to throw Mr. Khrushchev "on the rubbish heap of history."

Mr. Khrushchev's Visit to Hungary (April 1964)

Mr. Khrushchev arrived in Budapest on March 31 for a visit to Hungary, during which he made a number of speeches defending the Soviet view on peaceful coexistence and the primary importance of the economic development of the Communist countries.

Mr. Khrushchev said on April 6: "Some people criticize us by saying, 'You are thinking all the time about a better life, but these are anti-Marxist, bourgeois slogans.' The working people of our countries reply to such critics, 'What then did we make the revolution for? We did not fight in order to live worse after the working class came to power.' . . . There are people who say, 'And what about the world revolution? Are you ready to sacrifice the interests of the world revolution?' We resolutely reject this charge. . . . Our sympathies and our support are with our class brothers in the capitalist countries and with the peoples fighting for liberation, but we reject the theory according to which we should unleash a war against the capitalist States in the interests of world revolution. . . . We are against the export of revolution and against the export of counter-revolution. . . .

"There are people who criticize us for our stand on questions of peace and war. These people say, 'You are afraid of war.' I have replied more than once to these brave men, 'Only a child or a fool does not fear war.' . . . The Chinese leaders say, 'Even if world war starts, what of it? Half of mankind will be destroyed, but the other half will survive.' . . . What can one say of such views? Let the people judge for themselves. . . .

"Some people are blabbering that the Soviet Union and the C.P.S.U. are begging for peace from the imperialists. This, of course, is slander. . . . We do not rely on entreaties, but on our own strength. . . . Even the leaders of the largest imperialist State, the United States of America, have to reckon with the new balance of forces in the world. . . .

"In our foreign policy we have always abided by the Leninist principle of peaceful coexistence between States with different social systems. . . . This is a good basis, and we would like to see the question of 'Who prevails over whom?' generally settled otherwise than by war. The system which gives the greater freedom to the peoples, which gives them more material and cultural benefits, will win in the final count. . . ."

Mr. Khrushchev made his strongest attack on the Chinese leaders in a speech in Budapest on April 9, in which he described them as "persons who, while using leftist, ultra-revolutionary phrases as a cover and while proclaiming their loyalty to Marxism-Leninism, are in fact sliding down on a number of questions into the mire of Trotskyism and Great-China chauvinism." He also accused them of "irresponsibly gambling with the destinies of millions of people" and of "trying to impose upon the fraternal parties their adventurist anti-Leninist course and to establish their hegemony over the international Communist movement."

Chinese Rejection of Soviet Proposals for Conference (May–July 1964)

In a letter of May 7 the central committee of the Chinese party rejected all the proposals contained in the Soviet letter of March 7, and in effect suggested that the proposed world conference should be postponed indefinitely.

Rejecting any suggestion of a cessation of polemics, the letter stated: "Our Press has not yet finished replying to your open letter of July 14, 1963. We have not yet started—to say nothing of completing—our reply to the more than 2,000 anti-Chinese articles and other items which you published after your open letter." After accusing the Soviet Union of "uniting with U.S. imperialism, the common enemy of the people of the whole world," and of "opposing the national liberation movement, the proletarian revolution, and the dictatorship of the proletariat," it demanded: "How can you expect us and all other Marxist-Leninists to keep silent about these foul deeds of yours?"

In reply to the Soviet proposals for a conference, the letter said: "Judging by present circumstances, not only is it impossible to hold the two-party talks in May, but it will also be too early to hold them in October. We consider it more appropriate to postpone them till some time in the first half of next year, say May. And if either the Chinese or the Soviet party then considers that the time is still not ripe, they can be further postponed. . . . We maintain that a series of preparatory steps are necessary in order to make the international meeting of fraternal parties a success. . . . It may require perhaps four or five years, or even longer, to complete these preparations. . . ."

Reiterating the Chinese proposal that only 17 parties should take part in the preparatory meeting, the letter pointed out that in some of the countries mentioned in the Soviet letter (e.g. Australia and Brazil) the Communist Party had split into a "Marxist-Leninist" and a "revisionist" party, whilst in India, it asserted, "the Dange clique have degenerated into pawns of the Indian big bourgeoisie and big landlords and into renegades from Communism." In such cases the Soviet and Chinese parties differed as to which party should be invited, but in the Chinese view "the first consideration should be given to those fraternal parties which uphold Marxism-Leninism."

71

The Soviet party repeated its proposals for an early conference in its reply, dated June 15.

After claiming that "the overwhelming majority of the fraternal parties" favoured such a conference, the Soviet letter maintained that the Chinese party now opposed it "because you could not count on support for your ideological and political platform from a world Communist forum." The meeting of Communist leaders in Moscow in 1957, it pointed out, had unanimously decided, with the support of Mao Tse-tung, to "entrust the Communist Party of the Soviet Union with the function of convening meetings of the Communist and Workers' parties in consultation with the fraternal parties."

On the question of who should be entitled to attend, the letter maintained that "the anti-party groups in Australia, Brazil, Belgium, Ceylon, and certain other countries" were "made up of anti-party opposition elements expelled from Marxist-Leninist parties and fighting against lawfully elected central committees," and had been "joined by Trotskyists, Anarchists, and renegades and apostates of all kinds." In reply to the Chinese attack on the leadership of the Australian, Brazilian, and Indian parties, it said: "We emphatically reject the unworthy methods by which the leaders of one party, the Communist Party of China, lay claim to a special position in the Communist movement, to the right to pass judgment on parties as a whole and on their leaders, and arbitrarily to decide issues that are only for the working class of the given country to decide."

The Soviet letter concluded: "We reiterate our proposal that a preparatory conference should be convened and attended by representatives of the 26 parties nominated by the world meeting of Communist parties as members of the drafting commission in 1960 and representing the interests of Communists in all the main regions of the world. We consider it necessary to reach agreement with the fraternal parties on the specific date of such a conference in the immediate future. As it has done in the past, the C.P.S.U. central committee expresses its readiness to hold a bilateral meeting of representatives of the C.P.S.U. and the C.P.C. on any agreed date. . . ."

The Chinese reply (dated July 28) again rejected the Soviet proposals, saying in part:

"The Communist Party of China persists in its stand for an international meeting of the fraternal parties for unity on the basis of Marxism-Leninism, to be held after ample preparations, and we are firmly opposed to your schismatic meeting. The C.P.C. solemnly declares: We will never take part in any international meeting or any preparatory meeting for it which you call for the purpose of splitting the international Communist movement. . . .

"Since you have made up your minds, you will most probably call the meeting. Otherwise, if you break your word you will become a laughing-stock for centuries. . . . If you do not call the meeting, people will say that you have followed the advice of the Chinese and the Marxist-Leninist parties, and you will lose face. If you do, you will land yourselves in an impasse without any way out. . . . Dear comrades, we appeal to you once more to stop at the brink of the precipice, and not to attach too much importance to face. But if you refuse to listen and are determined to take the road to catastrophe, suit yourselves. . . ."

Soviet Proposal for Preparatory Conference—Invitation rejected by Chinese Party (July–August 1964)

The central committee of the Soviet party took a decisive step towards an open breach with the Chinese party on July 30, when it invited the 25 other parties which had formed the preparatory committee at the 1960 conference to send delegations to Moscow on Dec. 15 to begin preparations for a world conference in 1965.

The Soviet letter stated: "An absolute majority of the fraternal parties have spoken out in favour of the necessity for collective action to overcome the difficulties which have sprung up in our ranks. They advocate the holding of a new international meeting of representatives of the Communist and Workers' parties, and, moreover, many parties insist that the convening of the meeting must not be postponed for a long period. . . .

"At the 1957 meeting the fraternal parties unanimously adopted the following decision: 'Entrust the Communist Party of the Soviet Union with the function of convening meetings of the Communist and Workers' parties in consultation with the fraternal parties.' Up to the present, necessary consultations have been held . . . and the positions of all the Communist parties have become manifest. . . . Taking into consideration the clearly expressed will of the absolute majority of the fraternal parties, the C.P.S.U. considers that the time is ripe to begin preparatory work for convening an international meeting. We hold that a drafting committee should be convened before the end of this year.

"As it has already become clear in the process of preliminary exchange of views that the question of the composition of the drafting committee could become a new obstacle to its convening, we regard as the only reasonable way out the convening of the drafting committee with the same composition with which it worked during the preparations for the 1960 meeting, that is, comprising the representatives of the Communist and Workers' parties of the following 26 countries [which were then enumerated]. The C.P.S.U. invites the representatives of the fraternal parties listed above to come to Moscow by Dec. 15, 1964. . . .

"The meeting will not be called to condemn anyone, to 'excommunicate' anyone from the Communist movement and the Socialist camp, to attach insulting labels, or to throw irresponsible charges at one another. . . . We consider that the meeting should concentrate its efforts on finding out the things in common which unite all the fraternal parties, and on seeking ways to overcome the existing differences. . . . It is possible that . . . unanimity may not be reached on all questions at once . . . Nevertheless, we are deeply convinced that this would not mean the 'formalization' of the split or the creation of obstacles to the further seeking of ways to unity. . . .

"It is our deep conviction that there are no insurmountable obstacles to the international meeting starting its work as soon as drafts of documents are prepared by the drafting committee—about the middle of 1965. The representatives of all the 81 parties which participated in the 1960 meeting may take part in the international meeting. The refusal of this or that party to join in this collective work cannot serve as a ground for further delays. . . ."

The Chinese party rejected the invitation on Aug. 30.

The Chinese party's letter said: "You arbitrarily lay it down that a drafting committee shall be convened without the prior attainment of unanimous agreement through bilateral and multilateral talks by the Chinese and Soviet parties and all the other fraternal parties concerned. The members of the drafting committee must be the 26 parties you have designated, no more and no less. . . . You even decide before the convening of your appointed drafting committee that an international meeting shall be held in the middle of next year.

"Furthermore, you have the effrontery to declare in your letter that, whether or not the fraternal parties participate, the drafting committee you have designated shall open shop as scheduled, and that the international meeting unilaterally called by you shall begin on the day prescribed. Thus the day in December 1964 on which you convene your drafting committee will go down in history as the day of the great split in the international Communist movement. . . .

"What is there in common between yourselves and the world's Marxist-Leninists? Today the most urgent task before Communists and the revolutionary peoples of the world is to oppose U.S. imperialism and its lackeys. But you are bent on collusion with the U.S. imperialists and on seeking common ground with them. You have repeatedly indicated to U.S. imperialism that you want to disengage from all fronts of struggle against it. When U.S. imperialism recently launched its armed aggression against a fraternal Socialist country, the Democratic Republic of Vietnam, not only did you fail to declare explicit support for Vietnam in its struggle against U.S. aggression, but you even aided and abetted the aggressor by actively supporting the U.S. attempt to intervene in Vietnam through the United Nations. While you pursue this anti-Communist, anti-popular, anti-revolutionary line, how can Marxist-Leninists reach any agreement or take any common action with you? . . .

"Concerning the preparation and convening of an international meeting and its composition, we have repeatedly said that it is necessary to achieve unanimity of views through consultation among all the fraternal parties, including the old ones and those rebuilt or newly founded [i.e. pro-Chinese parties which had broken away from existing Communist parties, as in Australia, Belgium, Brazil, Ceylon, and India]. Otherwise, no matter what drafting committee or international meeting you convene, it will be illegal. . . ."

Intensification of Polemics (July–October 1964)

Polemics by both sides became increasingly virulent during the summer and autumn of 1964. On July 14 (the first anniversary of the Soviet party's open letter) the *People's Daily* and *Red Flag* published their ninth reply to it, which contained one of their most violent attacks to date on "Khrushchev's phoney Communism."

The Chinese papers wrote: "Khrushchev has carried out a series of revisionist policies serving the interests of the bourgeoisie and rapidly swelling the forces of capitalism in the Soviet Union. On the pretext of combating the personality cult, Khrushchev has defamed the dictatorship of the proletariat and the Socialist system, and thus paved the way for the restoration of capitalism in the Soviet Union. He has supported the degenerates in leading positions . . . [and] has accelerated the polarization of classes in Soviet society. Khrushchev sabotages the Socialist planned economy, applies the capitalist principle of profit, develops capitalist free competition, and undermines Socialist ownership by the whole people.

"Khrushchev is peddling bourgeois ideology and bourgeois liberty, equality, fraternity, and humanity, inculcating bourgeois idealism and metaphysics and the reactionary ideas of bourgeois individualism, humanism, and pacifism among the Soviet people, and debasing Socialist morality. The rotten bourgeois culture of the West is now fashionable in the Soviet Union, and Socialist culture is ostracized and attacked. . . . The broad masses of the Soviet workers, collective farmers, and intellectuals are seething with discontent against the oppression and exploitation practised by the privileged stratum. . . ."

Each side cited the U.S. bombing attacks on North Vietnamese naval bases on Aug. 5 in support of its case against the other. The Chinese letter of Aug. 30 accused the U.S.S.R. of supporting U.S. "aggression" in North Vietnam, whilst Mr. Khrushchev said in Prague on Sept. 4 that "our opponents are trying to profit by the difficulties created by the actions of the Chinese diversionists," citing in this connexion "the repeated aggressions of the U.S. imperialists in South-East Asia, their armed attacks on the Democratic Republic of Vietnam, and their intervention in the internal affairs of Laos."

Both sides had previously intensified their radio propaganda from the summer of 1963 onwards. It was reported in August 1963 that powerful transmitters recently established in north-west China and Albania were broadcasting propaganda to the U.S.S.R. and Eastern Europe, and a year later Moscow Radio was broadcasting in Chinese for 70 hours a week and Peking Radio in Russian for 63 hours.

V: THE POST-KHRUSHCHEV
PERIOD, 1964–66

Mr. Khrushchev was removed from his party and governmental posts on Oct. 14, 1964, and was replaced by Mr. Brezhnev as first secretary of the party and by Mr. Kosygin as Prime Minister. According to Western correspondents, Mr. Khrushchev was accused *inter alia* of reducing the ideological conflict with China to the level of a personal feud between himself and Mao Tse-tung and underestimating the speed of Chinese scientific progress, which permitted China to explode her first atomic bomb on Oct. 16.

Temporary Improvement in Sino-Soviet Relations
(October–December 1964)

Relations between the U.S.S.R. and China temporarily improved after Mr. Khrushchev's dismissal. It was announced on Oct. 16 that Mao Tse-tung and other Chinese leaders had sent "warm greetings" to Mr. Brezhnev and Mr. Kosygin, coupled with the hope that "the unbreakable friendship between the Chinese and Soviet peoples may continue to develop." Chou En-lai and six other leading Chinese Communists visited Moscow on Nov. 5–13 for the celebrations of the anniversary of the Bolshevik Revolution, and during their visit took part in talks with the Soviet leaders which were officially described as "frank and comradely." Addressing a public meeting on Nov. 6, at which Chou was present, Mr. Brezhnev called for unity in the world Communist movement, while indicating that the U.S.S.R. would continue Mr. Khrushchev's foreign policy.

Mr. Brezhnev said that the Soviet leaders considered it their duty to strengthen the unity of the Communist world, and that there was an "urgent necessity" for a new world conference of Communist parties; he made no reference, however, to Mr. Khrushchev's proposal for a preparatory meeting of 26 parties on Dec. 15. No Communist party or Government, he said, had the right to impose its will on other parties or countries; there could be different forms of Socialist society, and the choice between them might be determined by the political and economic conditions in the country concerned.

Describing the Soviet Union's foreign policy as "consistent and immutable," Mr. Brezhnev gave as its main features unity of the Socialist camp, support for national liberation movements, co-operation with the non-aligned countries, peaceful coexistence, and "delivering mankind from war." He gave a warning against "aggressive forces" and said that the Soviet Union would maintain its defence capability at the highest possible level so long as no agreement was reached on disarmament.

For several weeks after the fall of Mr. Khrushchev the Chinese and Soviet parties refrained from direct attacks on each other. Polemics nevertheless continued in indirect forms, the Chinese and Albanian Press attacking what was described as "Khrushchevism without Khrushchev," and the Soviet Press defending policies which had been attacked by the Chinese in the past.

Red Flag published on Nov. 20 a violent denunciation of Mr. Khrushchev, which summed up its main accusations against him as follows: (1) He had attacked Stalin on the pretext of combating the personality cult. (2) He had sought all-round co-operation with "U.S. imperialism." (3) He had weakened the Soviet Union's defences and tried to prevent China from developing her nuclear strength by signing the test-ban treaty. (4) He had obstructed revolutionary movements by advocating a peaceful transition to Socialism. (5) He had opposed and sabotaged national liberation movements. (6) He had supported the "renegade Tito clique." (7) He had tried to injure and undermine Albania. (8) He had spread calumnies against the Chinese party. (9) He had opposed the development of other Communist countries in the name of "mutual economic assistance." (10) He had made use of "political degenerates, renegades, and turncoats" to carry out disruptive activities against other Communist parties. (11) He had violated the principle of unanimity by playing the "patriarchal father-party role" and had summoned an "illegal" meeting to split the Communist movement. (12) He had pursued policies intended to lead the Soviet Union back to capitalism. In his dealings with China he had torn up several hundred agreements and contracts; recalled several hundred Soviet experts; organized frontier incidents; fomented subversive activities in Sinkiang; and incited and aided the "Indian reactionaries" to make armed attacks on China. Any attempt to revive "Khrushchevism without Khrushchev," the article concluded, would "end in a blind alley."

Pravda replied in part to the Chinese criticisms in an editorial on Dec. 6 which declared that the condemnation of the personality cult was "irreversible," and defended the theory that during the transition to Communism the dictatorship of the proletariat was replaced by "the State of the entire people." [This theory, put forward in the Soviet party's programme of 1961, had been attacked in the 19th of the Chinese party's "25 Points" of June 14, 1963—see page 47.]

Disagreements over Policy on Vietnam
(January–April 1965)

The escalation of the war in Vietnam in the early months of 1965 contributed greatly to widen the gap between the U.S.S.R. and China. Whereas the former made repeated efforts to bring about a negotiated settlement, the latter consistently opposed any suggestion of a compromise. Details of a number of secret Soviet peace moves were given in a letter from the Chinese Government and party which was published in the London *Observer* on Nov. 14.

According to this source, the U.S. Government expressed the hope in January that the U.S.S.R. would use its influence to persuade the North Vietnamese Government to stop supporting and arming the *Viet Cong* and to end attacks on South Vietnamese cities. These demands, which the Chinese letter described as "preposterous," were passed on to North Vietnam by the Soviet Government.

Mr. Kosygin paid a visit to Hanoi on Feb. 6–10, during which the U.S.A. began regular air raids on North Vietnam on Feb. 7. He flew on Feb. 10 to Peking, where he had talks with Mao Tse-tung and Chou En-lai; this was the first meeting between Mao and a Soviet leader since Mr. Khrushchev's visit to Peking in October 1959. According to the Chinese letter, "Comrade Kosygin stressed the need to help the U.S.A. 'find a way out of Vietnam.' We pointed out that since the U.S. imperialists were intensifying their aggression against Vietnam this was no time to negotiate . . . Comrade Kosygin expressed agreement with our views at the time, and stated that the new Soviet leadership 'would not bargain with others on this issue.' " He left Peking on Feb. 11, no communiqué on the talks being issued. On his return to the U.S.S.R. he said in a broadcast on Feb. 26 that the talks had "helped to clarify the possibility of further developing our relations."

The Soviet Government proposed to China and North Vietnam on Feb. 16 that an international conference on Indo-China should be held, and without waiting for the Chinese reply submitted this proposal to the French Government on Feb. 23. The U.S. Government, however, announced on Feb. 25 that it was "not contemplating any negotiations."

On April 3 the U.S.S.R. proposed a summit meeting of the Soviet, Chinese, and North Vietnamese leaders, contending that "the very fact of a demonstration of the unity of all the Socialist countries, and particularly of the U.S.S.R. and China . . . would constitute serious support for the Democratic Republic of [North] Vietnam and cool the ardour of the American militarists." The Chinese Government rejected this proposal, according to the letter, because "you intended to lure us into your trap through such a meeting so that you could speak on behalf of Vietnam and China in your international manoeuvres, and strengthen your position for doing a political deal with U.S. imperialism."

The Moscow Meeting of 19 Communist Parties
(March 1965)

Pravda announced on Dec. 13, 1964, that "on the basis of joint consultations that have taken place among fraternal parties, and with a view to making better preparations for the meetings of the drafting commission and the international conference of Communist and Workers' parties, the first meeting of the drafting commission has been fixed for March 1, 1965." This announcement was the first official intimation that the meeting of the 26 parties had been postponed.

The invitation was accepted by all the parties invited except those of China, Albania, Romania, North Korea, North Vietnam, Indonesia, and Japan; the Chinese party revealed on March 20, 1965, that it had received the invitation in November, but had not replied. Several of the parties which accepted the invitation, notably the British,

Cuban, Italian, and Polish parties, did so with reservations; in consequence the Soviet party was obliged to abandon its original intention that the commission should prepare a draft programme for a world conference, and the March 1 conference was officially described only as a "consultative meeting."

At the meeting, which was held in Moscow on March 1–5, some delegations were reported to have pressed for the adoption of a resolution fixing the date for a world conference and condemning Chinese interference with other parties; this was opposed by the Italian and British representatives, who contended that it would widen the split in the international movement. The statement finally adopted suggested a preliminary consultative conference of the 81 parties taking part in the 1960 meeting to discuss the question of a new international conference, and called for the discontinuation of "open polemics, which are in character unfriendly and degrading to the fraternal parties." The meeting also adopted a resolution condemning the U.S. air raids on North Vietnam.

Renewed Chinese Polemics (March 1965)

Direct attacks on the Soviet party began again in the Chinese Press on March 1, the day on which the Moscow meeting opened.

The *People's Daily* protested on March 1 against the recent publication in Moscow of a book called *The International Revolutionary Movement of the Working Class,* edited by Mr. Ponomarev, which, it said, attacked the Chinese party "in an all-round, systematic, and foul manner," and commented: "The fact that the editors of the book go to great pains to boost Khrushchev's revisionism is further proof that Khrushchev's downfall merely means a change of signboard, and that what is on sale in the shop remains the old wares of Khrushchevite revisionism. . . . The new anti-Chinese book once again reveals the hypocrisy of those who profess to reinforce the solidarity of the international Communist movement, but in reality . . . actually deepen the split. While talking about putting an end to the public debate, they intensify anti-Chinese agitation. . . ."

On March 4 the *People's Daily* published a number of recent extracts from the Soviet Press supporting "the line of the 'three peacefuls' and 'two entires'" (i.e., peaceful coexistence, peaceful competition, peaceful transition to Socialism, the State of the entire people, and the party of the entire people), which, it said, formed "the main content of Khrushchevite revisionism." It commented: "If the whole business of Khrushchevite revisionism is to be continued, then why oust Khrushchev? . . ."

The *People's Daily* published on March 23 its most violent attack on the new Soviet leadership to date, denouncing the Moscow meeting as "illegal" and "schismatic" and demanding that they should publicly renounce their "errors."

"By replacing Khrushchev," it declared, "the new leaders have merely changed the signboard and employed more subtle methods in order better to apply Khrushchevism. . . . [They] continue Khrushchev's policy of U.S.-Soviet co-operation for the domination of the world." Their policy could be described as "three shams and three realities"—"sham anti-imperialism but real capitulation, sham revolution but real betrayal, and sham unity but a real split." China, it stated, had no intention of accepting the "illegal and schismatic" Moscow meeting's appeal for a truce in polemics, and if the Soviet arguments could not be refuted in 9,000 years, "then we shall take 10,000 years."

Describing the Moscow meeting's protest against the bombing of North Vietnam as "a first-class farce," the *People's Daily* declared: "The new Soviet leaders are now loudly proclaiming their support for the revolutionary struggle of the people of South Vietnam, but in reality they are trying to gain political capital for their dealings with the U.S. imperialists and to carry out their plot for peace talks, in a futile attempt to extinguish the revolutionary struggle of the South Vietnamese people." In conclusion, it demanded that the Soviet leaders should publicly admit that the Moscow meeting was "illegal"; renounce "Khrushchevism," the "revisionist" line of the 20th and 22nd congresses, and the 1961 party programme; admit their errors in their dealings with the Chinese, Albanian, and other "Marxist-Leninist" parties; and undertake to return to Marxism-Leninism, proletarian internationalism, and the principles of the 1957 and 1960 declarations.

Chinese Student Demonstrations in U.S.S.R.—Anti-Soviet Demonstration in Peking (March–April 1965)

On March 4, about 2,000 Chinese and Vietnamese students again demonstrated outside the U.S. Embassy in Moscow. Although the Embassy was protected by about 1,000 mounted and foot police, the students broke through them and stoned the building; order was not restored until about 500 soldiers were called in to clear the street. A soldier lost an eye in the fighting, and several policemen and students were injured.

The Chinese Government protested against the "ruthless suppression" of the demonstration in a Note to the Soviet Union on March 6, demanding an apology and the punishment of those responsible; it alleged in particular that six injured students had been forcibly evicted from a Moscow hospital, although they needed treatment. In Peking students staged a protest demonstration outside the Soviet Embassy on March 6—the first demonstration of the kind in the Chinese capital since the Communist revolution.

The Soviet reply (March 12) categorically denied the Chinese allegations, maintaining that the demonstrators had attacked unarmed policemen with sticks and stones and seriously injured over 30 policemen and soldiers. A group of Chinese citizens, it declared, had afterwards demanded hospital treatment, and when a medical examination had established that they did not need it they had insulted the staff. The Note concluded with a warning that foreigners guilty of disturbing public order would be brought to trial and punished.

The Chinese Government's reply (March 16) rejected the Soviet Note, asserting that it "distorted the facts and reversed right and wrong."

The New China News Agency alleged on May 7 that the Soviet police had forcibly broken up a demonstration by Vietnamese students in Leningrad on April 3, injuring seven of the students and arresting 82.

Chinese Attacks on New Soviet Leaders (June–September 1965)

The Chinese Communist Party made its first direct attack on the Soviet leaders since the dismissal of Mr. Khrushchev in a long editorial published in the Peking *People's Daily* on June 14, 1965, which declared that they "have not departed from the essence of Khrushchev's policies—revisionism, great-Power chauvinism, and Soviet-American co-operation for the domination of the world." The Soviet party, which had refrained from open polemics against China since Mr. Khrushchev's removal from office, replied in an editorial in *Pravda* on June 19 deploring the Chinese attack, and appealing for international Communist unity against "U.S. aggression in Vietnam."

In an article published on Sept. 2 Marshal Lin Piao envisaged the "encirclement" of the U.S.A. and Western Europe by a world-wide revolutionary movement characterized by "people's wars" in the countries of Asia, Africa, and Latin America, and ridiculed "Khrushchev revisionists" for maintaining that "a single spark in any part of the globe may touch off a world nuclear conflagration and bring destruction to mankind." Describing the "Khrushchev line" of "peaceful coexistence, peaceful transition, and peaceful competition" as "rubbish," Marshal Lin said: "The essence of the general line of the Khrushchev revisionists is nothing other than the demand that all the oppressed peoples and nations and all the countries that have won independence should lay down their arms and place themselves at the mercy of the U.S. imperialists and their lackeys. . . ."

Soviet Reaction to New Sino-Indian Crisis
(September 1965)

During the war between India and Pakistan, the Chinese Government sent an ultimatum to India on Sept. 16 declaring that unless India dismantled all her military installations on the Sikkim border within three days it must "bear full responsibility for all the grave consequences," and at the same time moved up troops both on the Sikkim frontier and in Ladakh. China extended its ultimatum by another three days on Sept. 19, and in effect withdrew it on Sept. 21, when it claimed that the installations had been demolished, this allegation being denied by the Indian Government.

In the first Soviet comment on the Chinese ultimatum, *Pravda* stated on Sept. 23: "According to foreign news agencies, the handing over of the Chinese Notes has been accompanied by movements and concentrations of Chinese forces on India's borders. Reports of this kind cannot but evoke the concern of all those who are interested in the earliest liquidation of the Indo-Pakistani armed conflict, in consolidating the unity of all anti-imperialist forces, in restoring peace in South and South-East Asia, and in ending the machinations of imperialism in that region, especially U.S. aggression in Vietnam." The article was denounced as "calumnious" by the New China News Agency on Sept. 24.

Further Polemics (October–November 1965)

In reply to further Chinese attacks, *Pravda* published on Oct. 27 a full statement of the Soviet position.

After emphasizing that "one cannot win over the masses to the side of Socialism by words alone, even by the most revolutionary phrases," *Pravda* said that the Communist movement was made up of a number of detachments, each with its own special mission, and that the Soviet Union and other Socialist countries made their most useful contribution by building up their own prosperity and strength. "The Socialist countries," the article continued, "cannot replace other detachments of the liberation struggle in the solution of revolutionary tasks. They cannot replace the peoples of the young national States in the solution of tasks of the national liberation movement, or the working class and working people of the capitalist countries in the struggle for the overthrow of capitalism. This would be to force their will on other peoples. . . . Such actions might lead to the unleashing of world thermonuclear war, with all its severe consequences for all peoples. This would be for the Socialist countries to fail in their international obligations to the working people of the world, and would do irreparable damage to the cause. . . ."

A violent attack on the Soviet party, entitled "Refutation of the

New Leaders of the C.P.S.U. on 'United Action,' " appeared on Nov. 11 in the *People's Daily* and *Red Flag*.

The article asserted that the new Soviet leaders were "still pursuing Khrushchev's line, but with double-faced tactics more cunning and hypocritical than his," and were "allied with U.S. imperialism." They were "actively plotting new deals with the United States for the 'prevention of nuclear proliferation' and similar so-called 'disarmament' measures in an effort to maintain the monopoly of the two nuclear overlords, the Soviet Union and the United States, against China and all other independent countries," and in the previous September had "openly sided with India against China on the Sino-Indian border question" [see page 83].

"Some people ask," the article continued, "why is it that the Marxist-Leninists and the revolutionary people cannot take united action with the new leaders of the C.P.S.U., yet can unite with personages from the upper strata in the nationalist countries and strive for united action with them? . . . In the contemporary world, opposition to or alliance with U.S. imperialism constitutes the hallmark for deciding whether or not a political force can be included in the united front against the United States. . . . So far from opposing U.S. imperialism, the new leaders of the C.P.S.U. are allying themselves and collaborating with it to dominate the world."

Rejecting the Soviet proposal for united action on Vietnam, the article repeated the details of Soviet attempts to bring about peace negotiations. Soviet aid to North Vietnam, it continued, was "far from commensurate with the strength of the Soviet Union. They have ulterior motives in giving a certain amount of aid—they are trying to hoodwink the people at home and abroad, to keep the situation in Vietnam under their control, to gain a say on the Vietnam question, and to strike a bargain with U.S. imperialism on it." After denying Soviet allegations that China had obstructed the transit of Soviet military equipment for North Vietnam, the article rejected Soviet proposals for an end to open polemics, and declared that "we shall carry the debate to the finish."

In reply to Soviet statements that all the Communist countries had "a socio-economic system of the same type," the article asserted: "The report on the problems of industry by Kosygin at the recent plenary session of the central committee of the C.P.S.U. and the resolution which it adopted marked a big step along the road of the restoration of capitalism in the Soviet economy. [The resolution recommended greater freedom for individual enterprises, fuller use of bonus schemes, and increased use of the profit motive as an incentive to greater efficiency.] . . . In the countryside, too, the new leaders of the C.P.S.U. are accelerating the growth of capitalism, developing the private economy, enlarging the private plots, increasing the number of privately raised cattle, expanding the free market, and encouraging free trading. They are using a variety of economic and administrative measures to encourage and foster the growth of a new kulak economy. . . . Because they are the political representatives of the privileged bourgeois stratum in the Soviet Union, just as Khrushchev was, the new leaders of the C.P.S.U. pursue domestic and foreign policies which are not proletarian but bourgeois, not Socialist but capitalist. . . .

"Comrade Mao Tse-tung has often said to comrades from fraternal parties that if China's leadership is usurped by revisionists in the future, the Marxist-Leninists of all countries should resolutely expose and fight them, and help the working class and the masses of China to combat such revisionism. Taking the same stand, we consider it our bounden proletarian-internationalist duty firmly to expose the revisionist leadership of the C.P.S.U. . . ."

Pravda described the Chinese article on Nov. 16 as "saturated with impermissible, utterly groundless, slanderous, and provocative fabrications," and replied to it at length in an editorial on Nov. 28.

"Demonstrating its goodwill and striving for the cohesion of all revolutionary forces, our party has refrained for over a year from open polemics," the *Pravda* editorial said: "This is not because it had nothing to say. . . . Unfortunately the Soviet Communist Party and other parties met with no positive response from the Chinese Communist Party leaders. . . . The policy of political and organizational division, a policy of splitting the Communist movement, is now actually put forward in opposition to the stand of those parties favouring unity of action. . . . To oppose unity now and call for division is to act contrary to the interests of the revolution. . . . The Soviet Communist Patry has always been implacably opposed to any opportunist who, donning various masks—including those of 'super-revolutionaries'—has tried to divert the Communist movement from the right road. . . ."

Soviet Letter to Other Communist Parties
(February 1966)

The central committee of the Soviet Communist Party was reported on Feb. 14, 1966, to have recently sent a letter to the other Communist parties of Eastern Europe on its relations with the Chinese party. What was believed to be an authentic copy of the letter was published on March 22 in the Hamburg newspaper *Die Welt*, and is summarized below; this gave details of Soviet proposals for co-operation with China and of Soviet aid to North Vietnam, and accused the Chinese party of wishing to bring about war between the Soviet Union and the United States.

"Since the plenum of October 1964," the letter stated, "the C.P.S.U. central committee has done everything possible to normalize relations with the C.P.C. [Communist Party of China]. . . . In endeavouring to create a favourable political atmosphere, the C.P.S.U. central committee has unilaterally discontinued open polemics. . . . In the negotiations with the Chinese party-Government delegation headed by Chou En-lai [in November 1964—see page 77] . . . we submitted an extensive programme for normalizing Chinese-Soviet relations at both the party and the State level. This programme included proposals on implementing bilateral meetings of delegations of the C.P.S.U. and the C.P.C. on the highest level, on the mutual discontinuation of polemics, concrete proposals on extending Chinese-Soviet trade and scientific, technical, and cultural co-operation, and on co-ordinating the foreign policy activities of the C.P.R. [Chinese People's Republic] and the U.S.S.R. . . . The C.P.C. central committee completely ignored the proposal on a bilateral meeting on the highest level. The C.P.C. leadership failed to accede to an expansion of economic, technical, and cultural co-operation, and even took additional steps to further curtail such co-operation. . . .

"The anti-Soviet course has now become an inseparable part of the entire ideological work of the C.P.C., both within and outside the country. . . . The Chinese leadership increasingly intensifies subversive activities against the Soviet State and social order. Peking Radio beams articles and material to the U.S.S.R. in an attempt to pit various strata of the Soviet people against one another. . . . Direct appeals are being made to engage in political action against the C.P.S.U. central committee and the Soviet Union.

"The C.P.R. leadership propagates ever more obstinately the thesis of potential military clashes between China and the Soviet Union. On Sept. 29, 1965, Chen Yi, Foreign Minister of the C.P.R., at a press conference in Peking spoke utterly falsely of a possible 'co-ordination' of Soviet actions in the north of China with the aggressive war of the United States against the C.P.R. . . . The idea is obstinately suggested to the Chinese people that it is necessary to prepare for a military conflict with the U.S.S.R. The C.P.S.U. central committee has already informed the fraternal parties that the Chinese side is provoking border conflicts. Such conflicts have again increased in recent months. . . . The Chinese Government refuses to resume the negotiations suspended in May 1964 on a precise delimitation of the border. It obviously prefers to leave this question unsettled. At the same time, allegations are being spread to the effect that the Soviet Union unlawfully holds Chinese territory in the Far East. . . .

"The attitude of the C.P.R. leadership towards the struggle of the D.R.V. [Democratic Republic of Vietnam] . . . against the U.S. aggression is currently causing great damage to the joint cause of the countries of Socialism," the letter continued. "The Soviet Union delivers large quantities of weapons to the D.R.V., including rocket installations, anti-aircraft artillery, aeroplanes, tanks, coastal guns, warships, and other items. In 1965 alone weapons and other war material worth about 500,000,000 roubles were placed at the disposal of the D.R.V. The D.R.V. is receiving support in the training of pilots, rocket personnel, tank drivers, artillerymen, etc. Our military aid is being rendered to the extent the Vietnamese leadership itself thinks necessary. The Soviet Union grants extensive military and material support to the National Liberation Front of South Vietnam.

"The C.P.S.U. has proposed to the Chinese leaders more than once that joint action to support Vietnam be organized, but the Chinese leadership opposed such action. . . . Our party has proposed twice that the representatives of the three parties—the Vietnamese Party of Labour, the C.P.S.U., and the C.P.C.—meet at the highest level to achieve agreement on co-ordinated action for aid to the D.R.V. These proposals, which were received by the Politburo of the Vietnamese Party of Labour with approval, were not accepted by the Chinese leaders. At the same time, the C.P.C. leadership hindered the implementation of the agreement of the Government of the U.S.S.R. with the Government of the D.R.V. on an immediate increase in military aid for the D.R.V. The C.P.C. leaders did not permit Soviet transport planes with weapons to fly over C.P.R. territory. Chinese personalities also placed obstacles in the way of the transportation of war material to Vietnam by rail. . . .

"From all this it becomes clear that the Chinese leaders need a lengthy Vietnamese war to maintain international tensions, to represent China as a 'besieged fortress.' There is every reason to assert that it is one of the goals of the policy of the Chinese leadership on the Vietnam question to originate a military conflict between the U.S.S.R. and the United States . . . so that they may, as they say themselves, 'sit on the mountain and watch the fight of the tigers.' New facts constantly prove the readiness of the Chinese leaders to sacrifice the interests of the national liberation movement to their chauvinist big-Power plans. . . . The nationalist big-Power policy of the Chinese leaders has led to the fact that the C.P.R. recently has suffered a number of serious setbacks on the international scene. The actions of the C.P.C. leaders have led to a spreading of mistrust of the C.P.R., even in countries which until very recently were regarded as its friends. This became especially clear on the African continent and in a number of Asian countries. . . .

"The well-known disruptive agitation of the C.P.C. leaders in the Communist movement has become very intensive. . . . The Chinese leaders have established factional groups in approximately 30 countries. . . . By supporting these groups and promoting their disruptive activity, the Chinese leaders openly interfere in the internal affairs of other Communist parties. . . .

"The role of the ideological-theoretical platform of the Chinese leadership is quite plain. Its exclusive purpose is to serve the nationalistic big-Power policy of the Chinese leadership. . . . The course towards Socialist revolution . . . has been replaced by a course towards a world war. These ideas were most completely explained in the recent article by Lin Piao. . . .

"The C.P.S.U. . . . has always recognized armed as well as peaceful forms of struggle of the working class for power. . . . The Chinese leaders, in contrast, derive from the whole arsenal of forms of struggle only one—armed revolt, war. . . . The efforts of the C.P.C. leaders to force all parties of the non-Socialist countries to accept the goal of an immediate revolution independent of actual conditions means in effect to try to force upon the Communist movement putschist, conspiratory tactics. These tactics, however, offer the imperialist bourgeoisie the opportunity to bleed the revolutionary Communist and workers' movement, and to expose the leadership and activists of a number of Communist parties to destruction. . . ."

[This passage referred to the attempted coup on Oct. 1, 1965, by the pro-Chinese Communist Party of Indonesia, after the suppression of which at least 150,000 Communists, including most of the party's leaders, were massacred.]

"The Chinese leaders," the letter went on, "emphasize the idea that international tension is favourable for revolution by force, that it creates favourable prerequisites for their struggle. They come forth with statements that can hardly be assessed as anything but provocatory. Thus Chen Yi declared in one of his latest interviews: 'If the U.S. imperialists have decided to force a war of aggression upon us, then we would welcome it. . . . We would welcome it if they came as early as tomorrow.' And what should one think, for example, of the statement of the same Chen Yi: 'With the help of the atom bomb one may destroy one or two generations of people. But the third generation will rise to offer resistance. And peace will be restored.' . . . Our people, who have taken up arms more than once to defend the achievements

87

of the revolution, are not afraid of threats from imperialism. We are, however, definitely against adventures, against urging people towards nuclear world war. . . .

"We believe that the hegemonic activities of the Chinese leaders," the letter concluded, "are aimed at subordinating the policy of Socialist countries, the international Communist and workers' movement, and the national liberation movement to their great-Power interests. . . . It is not without intention that the Chinese leaders, while criticizing the other fraternal parties and Socialist countries because of their alleged insufficient revolutionary spirit and indecisiveness in the fight against imperialism, show extraordinary caution in their own practical deeds. . . ."

The 23rd Soviet Party Congress (March–April 1966)

The Chinese party announced on March 23 that it had refused an invitation to send a delegation to the 23rd congress of the Soviet Communist Party, and published its letter rejecting the invitation.

The Chinese letter alleged that the Soviet leadership had sent a letter to other Communist parties "instigating them to join you in opposing China," and had spread "rumours" that China was obstructing Soviet aid to North Vietnam and encroaching on Soviet territory. The Chinese Communist Party, it continued, had sent delegations to the last three congresses, but "at the 20th Congress of the C.P.S.U. [Communist Party of the Soviet Union] you suddenly lashed out at Stalin. Stalin was a great Marxist-Leninist. In attacking Stalin you were attacking Marxism-Leninism, the Soviet Union, Communist parties, China, the people, and all the Marxist-Leninists of the world. At the 22nd Congress you adopted an out-and-out revisionist programme, made a wild public attack on Albania, and reproached the Chinese Communist Party, so that the head of our delegation had to leave for home while the congress was only halfway through.

"Russia is the native land of Leninism," the letter declared, "and used to be the centre of the international working-class movement. After Stalin's death the leaders of the C.P.S.U., headed by Khrushchev, gradually revealed their true features as betrayers of Lenin and Leninism. . . . The leadership of the C.P.S.U. has become the centre of modern revisionism. Over the last 10 years we have made a series of efforts in the hope that you would return to the path of Marxism-Leninism. Since Khrushchev's downfall we have advised the new leaders of the C.P.S.U. on a number of occasions to make a fresh start . . . but you have not shown the slightest repentance. Since coming to power the new leaders of the C.P.S.U. have gone farther and farther down the road of revisionism, splittism, and great-Power chauvinism."

The letter went on to accuse the Soviet party of "pursuing U.S.-Soviet collaboration for the domination of the world"; of "acting in co-ordination with the United States in its plot for peace talks, vainly attempting to sell out the struggle of the Vietnamese people against U.S. aggression and . . . to drag the Vietnam question into the orbit of Soviet-U.S. collaboration"; and of "actively trying to build a ring of encirclement around Socialist China." The letter concluded: "Since you have gone so far, the Chinese Communist

Party, as a serious Marxist-Leninist party, cannot send its delegation to attend this congress of yours."

In his report to the congress, which met in Moscow from March 29 to April 8, Mr. Brezhnev said that the party sincerely wanted friendship with China, and was "ready at any moment, jointly with the Communist Party of China, to re-examine the existing differences with the object of finding ways of overcoming them." He also expressed support for a new international Communist conference "when the conditions for it are ripe."

VI: THE PERIOD OF THE CULTURAL REVOLUTION, 1966–69

A new turning-point in the struggle was reached with the 11th plenary session of the Chinese party's central committee, held on Aug. 1–12, 1966, which officially endorsed the policy of the "Great Proletarian Cultural Revolution." A long communiqué issued on Aug. 13 reaffirmed the party's hostility to Soviet "revisionism," and its refusal to co-operate with the U.S.S.R. on the Vietnamese question. Although the communiqué merely repeated views which had frequently been expressed in the past, its adoption by the central committee gave an official character to what *Le Monde* described as "the definitive break with the Soviet party."

The statement rejected the Chinese contention that the purpose of Soviet aid was to make North Vietnam so dependent on it that she would have to yield to Soviet pressure in favour of unconditional negotiations with the United States, and denounced China's opposition to joint action as purely negative. It suggested that China feared that increased foreign aid to North Vietnam might lead to further escalation of the war and endanger China's own security, and commented that this resembled the arguments used by Mr. Khrushchev to justify Soviet passivity. Any agreement on joint action, however, must be conditional on Soviet assurances of "a maximum increase in weapons aid to the Vietnamese, positive aid to the Vietnamese to the very last, without

90

deceiving them in their expectations, and a total ban on separate secret dealings with the United States." The statement suggested that the Soviet leadership was divided between "revisionists" who favoured a compromise settlement in Vietnam and "anti-revisionist elements," and advocated that foreign Communist parties should continue their struggle against "revisionism" while promoting the development of "anti-revisionist" policies within the Soviet party.

The widening of the breach between the two parties in the past four years was illustrated by the contrast between the communiqué and that issued after the central committee's previous plenary session, on Sept. 28, 1962 (see Chapter IV). The 1962 communiqué declared that "the modern revisionists are represented by the Tito clique"; stated that it was China's policy to "develop relations of friendship, mutual assistance, and co-operation with the U.S.S.R.";and expressed support for the 1957 Moscow declaration and the 1960 Moscow statement. The new communiqué referred to the Soviet leaders as heading the "modern revisionists"; adopted a violently hostile attitude towards the U.S.S.R.; and made no mention of the 1957 declaration and the 1960 statement. Among those most violently denounced as "revisionists" during the next few months were Teng Hsiao-ping, who had headed the Chinese delegation at the 1960 Moscow Conference and the 1963 Moscow talks, and Peng Chen, who had been a member of the Chinese delegation on both occasions and had also represented China at the Bucharest Conference.

Demonstrations outside Soviet Embassy in Peking (August 1966)

Demonstrations by thousands of students and school-children, organized as "Red Guards of the Cultural Revolution," began in Peking on Aug. 20. The Red Guards repeatedly demonstrated outside the Soviet Embassy, carrying portraits of Mao Tse-tung and Stalin, and renamed the street leading to it "Struggle against Revisionism Street." On Aug. 20 a senior Soviet diplomat was prevented by mobs from leaving the Embassy for an official appointment. The Soviet Government strongly protested to the Chinese Embassy in Moscow on Aug. 26 against this "direct breach of generally recognized norms of international law," and demanded the immediate ending of the "hooliganism" outside the Soviet Embassy in Peking. The Chinese authorities retorted by organizing mass demonstrations outside the Embassy on Aug. 29–30, during which thousands of Red Guards beat drums and shouted anti-Soviet slogans; the Embassy gates were strongly guarded by troops and police, however, and no incidents occurred. A statement by the Soviet Communist Party on Aug. 31 described the "outrages" outside the Embassy as "a new serious step damaging the cause of the unity of the international Communist movement." The East German Embassy had previously made a strong protest on Aug. 28 after its military attaché and his family had been assaulted by Red Guards.

A statement issued by the Soviet Communist Party on Aug. 31 condemned the Chinese party's communiqué of Aug. 13 and the "outrages" outside the Embassy as "a new serious step damaging the cause of the unity of the international Communist movement" and rendering "a particularly big service to imperialism and reaction."

During the first half of September the Soviet Press concentrated on reporting criticisms of Chinese policy by other Communist parties, but on Sept. 20 *Izvestia* published an editorial describing recent developments in China as "not only a tragedy for the Chinese people but an unprecedented discreditation of the ideas of Marxism-Leninism." After stating that China had outlawed herself from the world Communist movement, the editorial expressed confidence that "in the end healthy forces of the Communist Party of China must lead the country back to the true path of Marxism-Leninism."

Soviet Criticisms of Chinese Foreign Policy
(September–December 1966)

From September onwards the Soviet Government and Communist Party adopted an increasingly critical attitude towards the Chinese party's foreign policies. In reply to repeated Chinese allegations of "collusion" between the Soviet Union and the United States, Soviet spokesmen suggested that the Chinese Government, while itself developing contacts with the U.S.A., was seeking to provoke a conflict between the United States and the Soviet Union.

This theory was first put forward on Sept. 21 by *Izvestia*, in an article composed entirely of quotations from Western newspapers. It quoted without comment the view attributed to "highly-placed Americans" that "if one set aside Peking's verbal escalations, we have not yet seen any Chinese presence in the Vietnam conflict," and noted that a statement said to have been made by Marshal Chen Yi (who had succeeded Chou En-lai as Foreign Minister in 1958) to a group of visiting Japanese politicians, that he did not exclude the possibility of talks with the United States about a negotiated settlement of the Vietnamese question, had never been officially denied in Peking. The article also quoted reports that "clearly formulated conditions" had been drawn up at the Sino-American ambassadorial contacts in Warsaw on ways of avoiding a clash between China and the United States in Vietnam; U.S. pilots, it alleged, had strict orders to keep clear of the Chinese frontier, and the Chinese Government had agreed to consider any "errors" which might take place as "regrettable incidents."

At the celebrations in Peking on Oct. 1 of the 17th anniversary of the founding of the Chinese People's Republic the diplomatic representatives of the Soviet Union and the Eastern European countries, with the exception of Romania, left the rostrum when Marshal Lin Piao declared that "imperialism headed by the United States, and modern revisionism with leaders of the Soviet Communist Party at its centre, are actively plotting peace talk swindles for stamping out the rising flames of the Vietnamese people's national revolutionary war." On Nov. 7 the Chinese representatives walked out from the celebrations of the anniversary of the Russian Revolution in Moscow when Marshal Malinovsky (then Soviet Defence Minister) said that China's divisive influence in the Socialist camp "encouraged U.S. imperialism to new crimes." A similar incident occurred at the May Day parade in Red Square on May 1, 1967, when Marshal Grechko (Marshal Malinovsky's successor) said that "the hour of failure for the aggressors' gamble in Vietnam would come much sooner if there existed unity of action of all the Socialist countries, including China."

In the strongest Soviet attack on Chinese policies published since the fall of Mr. Khrushchev, *Pravda* openly accused the Chinese leaders on Nov. 27, 1966, of attempting to promote war between the Soviet Union and the United States, and suggested that the Cultural Revolution was directed against those Chinese Communists who opposed this policy.

"The duplicity of the policy of the Chinese leaders is increasingly showing itself in the international arena," *Pravda* said. "On the one hand, they try to impose on the fraternal parties a course that would lead to a continuous aggravation of the international situation and ultimately to war, allegedly in the name of the world revolution. On the other, they pursue a policy which allows them to remain on the sidelines of the struggle against imperialism. While describing all Soviet-American contacts as 'collusion,' the Chinese leaders do not miss any chance to develop their relations with capitalist countries, including the United States. Their 'escalation,' which is purely verbal, is accompanied in the Chinese Press by an intense exploitation of the theme of tension on the Sino-Soviet frontier. It is therefore not surprising that the bourgeois Press publishes reports of a tacit agreement between China, the United States, and other capitalist countries, which are very satisfied with Peking's present policy. . . .

"Mao Tse-tung and his entourage could not disregard the fact that the party cadres who went through the school of revolution, despite the anti-Soviet campaign of the past years, came to realize increasingly all the harm caused to China by the split with the Soviet Union and other Socialist countries. It is difficult to deceive them with fabrications about Soviet 'collusion' with the United States and the 'restoration of capitalism' in our country. That is why Mao Tse-tung and his group chose the road of defamation and destruction of the party cadres, or best representatives of the working class and the intellectuals, using for this purpose a section of the students and schoolchildren and the military and administrative apparatus. . . ."

Marshal Chen Yi, on the other hand, suggested in an interview published in a Brazilian paper on Dec. 11 that the Soviet Union was planning to attack China in alliance with the United States.

"The Russians have 13 divisions on the Chinese frontier which have been moved from Eastern Europe," said Marshal Chen Yi, "but we are not afraid of a Soviet-American attack. The Chinese people are ready for war and confident of final victory. We now have the atomic bomb and also rockets. We are not afraid of nuclear or conventional war, or any other kind of war that the Americans may invent." He went on to suggest that the aim of Soviet policy was the formation of "a new Holy Alliance" with the United States for a joint attack on China, the Russians attacking from the north and the Americans from the south, and added: "For this reason China is preparing for war, and all the nuclear bombs which fall on China will be returned with interest. . . ."

First Official Soviet Attack on Mao Tse-tung (December 1966)

The central committee of the Soviet Communist Party, at a plenary session on Dec. 12–13, adopted a resolution condemning the policy of "Mao Tse-tung and his group." This was the first time that Mao had been attacked by name in an official statement of the Soviet party.

"The anti-Soviet great-Power policy of Mao Tse-tung and his group has entered a new and dangerous phase," the resolution said. "The policy of the present leaders of the Chinese Communist Party in the international arena has nothing in common with Marxism-Leninism, and their actions objectively assist imperialism. The central committee finds it necessary to expose resolutely the anti-Leninist views and the great-Power nationalist course of the present Chinese leaders, and to intensify the struggle in defence of Marxism-Leninism and the general line laid down in Moscow by the conferences in 1957 and 1960. . . . The central committee expresses its agreement with the fraternal Marxist-Leninist parties on the appearance at the present time of favourable conditions for the convening of a new conference of representatives of the Communist and Workers' parties, which must be well prepared in the course of mutual consultations between the parties. . . ."

Almost all the members of the party's Politburo and Secretariat addressed a series of meetings of party members in the leading cities of the Soviet Union during the first half of January 1967, at which they explained the significance of the central committee's resolution. Speaking at Gorky on Jan. 13, Mr. Brezhnev said that the Cultural Revolution was "a great tragedy for all true Chinese Communists, with whom we express our profound sympathy"; he emphasized that in denouncing the ideology and policy of "Mao Tse-tung and his group," the Soviet party was not attacking China or the Chinese party, which it hoped would return to the path of internationalism.

Expulsion of Foreign Students and Soviet Journalists from China—Expulsion of Chinese Students from U.S.S.R. (September–December 1966)

Foreign embassies in Peking were requested on Sept. 20 to repatriate all foreign students by Oct. 10, as their teachers were too busy with the Cultural Revolution to attend to them. The Soviet Government thereupon announced on Oct. 7 that, as the Sino-Soviet agreement on cultural co-operation provided for the exchange of students on a basis of reciprocity, all Chinese students must leave the Soviet Union by Oct. 31, but that it would consider resuming the exchange of students as soon as the Chinese Government was prepared to do so. After the Soviet Embassy in Peking had refused on Oct. 22 to accept a Chinese Note protesting against the expulsion of the Chinese students, demonstrations by Red Guards began outside the Embassy on Oct. 23 and continued for several days.

A Soviet Note of Oct. 27 protested against the conduct of the Red Guards, who, it stated, had blocked the entrance to the Embassy, threatened Soviet diplomats, and indulged in "unprintable abuse, obscene gestures and poses, and spitting." It commented that "it is impossible to avoid the impression that flagrant violations of universally recognized principles of relations between States, elementary standards of international law, and the immunity of missions are becoming something of a standard practice in China."

The Chinese reply (Nov. 1) rejected the Soviet protest as "absurd and unreasonable" and asserted that the Soviet Government, "acting in collusion with U.S. imperialism," had "intensified its efforts to aggravate Sino-Soviet

95

relations and expelled all Chinese students from the Soviet Union without reason." The Note went on: "This act did not fail to arouse the unbounded indignation of large numbers of Chinese. It was a perfectly just and revolutionary act for the Chinese revolutionary youth to mass spontaneously in Struggle against Revisionism Street near the Soviet Embassy and stick up large posters protesting against the unreasonable expulsion of Chinese students. Since the coming to power of the new leaders of the Soviet Communist Party, to say nothing of the previous period, you have collaborated with the United States, India, and Japan to encircle China. You have perfidiously and arbitrarily torn up the agreements between China and the Soviet Union and taken a series of steps tending constantly to aggravate relations between the two countries. You have gone even farther than Khrushchev on the road of revisionism and splittism. . . ."

The Chinese Foreign Ministry demanded on Dec. 16 that three of the six Soviet correspondents resident in Peking should leave the country within 10 days, as there were only three Chinese correspondents in Moscow; it also alleged that they had spread "rumours and slanders" about the Cultural Revolution "to meet the needs of the Soviet revisionist leading clique for attacking China." The Soviet Foreign Ministry commented on Dec. 23 that the question of limiting the number of correspondents had never before been raised by either side, and reserved the right to take appropriate measures if necessary against the Chinese correspondents, whose reports were full of "slanderous inventions."

The Red Square Incident (January–February 1967)

All Chinese studying abroad were recalled to China in January 1967 in order to take part in the Cultural Revolution. One party of students returning from France and Finland via Moscow became engaged in a brawl in Red Square on Jan. 25, of which widely differing accounts were given by the Soviet and Chinese Governments.

According to the Soviet version, the students, who were accompanied by Chinese Embassy officials, lined up in front of the entrance to Lenin's mausoleum and chanted quotations from Mao Tse-tung, while 700 or 800 people waited in the freezing cold. When a policeman asked them to stop holding up the queue they began shouting "hysterically," and one of them struck a woman in the face. The others then began assaulting the bystanders, one woman being trampled on, until people in the queue linked arms, formed a line, and pushed the Chinese back to their buses. At a press conference on Jan. 28 a Soviet spokesman said that there were only two or three policemen near the mausoleum at the time, and not more than 10 in the whole of Red Square, whilst eye-witnesses of the incident denied that any of the Chinese had been injured.

96

A Chinese Foreign Ministry statement, on the other hand, asserted that "69 Chinese students returning from Europe via Moscow proceeded in an orderly and neat column to Lenin's mausoleum and Stalin's tomb to lay wreaths. . . . When they were reading out quotations from Chairman Mao Tse-tung, the Soviet Government called out the two or three hundred soldiers, policemen, and plain-clothes men planted there in advance to encircle and savagely assault them, injuring over 30 of them with four seriously wounded, of whom one is in a critical state with broken ribs." After denouncing "this Fascist atrocity," and comparing "the Soviet revisionist ruling clique" to the German, Italian, and Japanese Fascists, Chiang Kai-shek, Tsar Nicholas II, paper tigers, and "a few flies freezing to death in the whirling snow," the statement expressed confidence that the Soviet people would "rise in rebellion against the revisionist rulers, dismiss them from office, seize power from them, and smash the revisionist rule to smithereens."

In a Note of Jan. 26 the Soviet Foreign Ministry protested against the students' conduct, and demanded that the Chinese Embassy should ensure that "Chinese citizens on Soviet territory conduct themselves in a seemly manner." A counterprotest delivered by the Chinese Embassy on the same day demanded an apology and the severe punishment of those responsible for "this grave and premeditated crime."

Two of the students alleged to have been injured addressed foreign correspondents at a press conference at the Chinese Embassy on Jan. 28, from which Soviet and U.S. journalists were excluded. One of them, who according to the *Times* correspondent had "a suspicion of a black eye," asserted that the police had "kicked me in the lower part of the body so that I bled from my injury." The other appeared wearing a gauze mask over his face, to give the impression that he had been gravely injured; in the course of an impassioned denunciation of "the Fascist ordures Brezhnev and Kosygin," however, he ripped off the mask, revealing that his face was quite unharmed.

The Soviet Foreign Ministry asked the Chinese Chargé d'Affaires on Feb. 3 to remove the display cases outside the Chinese Embassy, on which photographs of the incident in Red Square and texts denouncing Soviet leaders were on show. After this request had been refused the cases were removed by Soviet civilians later the same day.

A Chinese Government statement asserted that 160 to 170 plain-clothes policemen had entered the Embassy grounds, forcibly removed the cases, and assaulted 31 of the Embassy staff, seriously injuring three of them. "Only Hitler's Fascist Germany and U.S. imperialism, the common enemy of the people of the world," the statement continued, "are capable of perpetrating this outrage committed by the Soviet revisionist ruling clique in brazenly violating the most elementary principles guiding international relations. It is entirely the making of the Soviet revisionist ruling clique that Sino-Soviet relations have been damaged to such a serious extent. . . ." Soviet spokesmen said that about 30 private individuals, "incensed by the materials displayed in the cases," had torn them down without entering the Embassy grounds, and that members of the Embassy staff had attacked them with their fists.

New Demonstrations outside Soviet Embassy in Peking
—Expulsion of Soviet and Chinese Diplomats
(January–March 1967)

The Moscow incident of Jan. 25 was followed by the most violent outburst of anti-Soviet propaganda ever published in Communist China. A typical example was an editorial entitled *Hit back hard at the Rabid Provocations of the Filthy Soviet Revisionist Swine!*, which appeared in the *People's Daily* on Jan. 27 and stated *inter alia:*

"Listen, you handful of filthy Soviet revisionist swine! The Chinese people, who are armed with Mao Tse-tung's thought, are not to be bullied! The debt of blood you owe must be paid! . . . How closely does your atrocious, bloody repression against the Chinese students resemble the atrocities committed by the Tsar, by Hitler, and by the Ku Klux Klan! This clearly shows that what you are practising in the Soviet Union is in fact the most reactionary and most savage Fascist dictatorship. . . ."

Demonstrations of unprecedented violence began outside the Soviet Embassy in Peking during the evening of Jan. 26. Huge crowds, which included armed soldiers, spat at and molested people entering or leaving the Embassy, threw paint over their cars and banged them with sticks, and hurled litter and burning torches over the fence, creating a danger of fire. The Embassy gates and fence were plastered with anti-Soviet posters, and effigies of Mr. Brezhnev and Mr. Kosygin were hung from trees. Powerful loudspeakers blared out anti-Soviet slogans day and night, preventing the Embassy staff from sleeping. Western correspondents, mistaken for Russians, had difficulty in escaping the violence of the mob.

Although the Soviet Foreign Ministry presented a strong protest to the Chinese Embassy in Moscow on Jan. 29, demanding that the Embassy should be protected and compensation paid for damage done to the building, the demonstrations became increasingly violent. Soviet diplomats were besieged in their car by Red Guards for 16 hours on Feb. 2, and on the following day Soviet specialists returning from North Vietnam were mobbed. A second Soviet protest of Feb. 4 warned the Chinese Government that "the restraint and patience of

98

Soviet men and women are not without limit," and that "the Soviet Union reserves the right to take steps, which will be guided by the situation, for the protection of the safety of its citizens and its lawful interests."

The wives and children of the Soviet Embassy staff were evacuated from Peking in three parties on Feb. 4–6. Those who left on Feb. 4 were jeered at by Red Guards at the airport, and on the following day the second party was prevented from boarding the aircraft for six hours by Red Guards, who broke into the bus taking them to the airport and on their arrival there struck them and spat at them. The most violent scenes took place on Feb. 6, when women, some of them carrying babies, and children were forced by a howling mob of Red Guards to crawl under portraits of Mao and Stalin. Soviet and other European diplomatists, including Mr. Donald Hopson (the British Chargé d'Affaires) and M. Lucien Paye (the French Ambassador), were roughly handled when they tried to protect the women and children, and Soviet officials returning to the Embassy were attacked, one group being held prisoners in their bus for 12 hours. Demonstrators broke down the Embassy gates, and paraded through the grounds waving signs threatening physical violence.

In the evening of Feb. 6 the Chinese Foreign Ministry notified the Soviet Embassy that its officials were forbidden to leave the Embassy compound, as otherwise their security could not be guaranteed, and for some days the Embassy was under a virtual stage of siege. Eastern European diplomats who delivered food to their Soviet colleagues on Feb. 7 were warned the following day that their safety could not be guaranteed if they went near the Embassy. Ignoring this warning, the diplomats supervised the delivery at the Embassy on Feb. 9 of food supplies which had been flown in from Moscow.

In a third protest Note, the Soviet Government stated on Feb. 9:

"The steps taken by the Chinese authorities may signify either a deliberate intention to undermine relations between the People's Republic of China and the Soviet Union, or inability on the part of these authorities to ensure in their country elementary conditions for the life and work of the representatives of a State which maintains normal diplomatic relations with the People's Republic of China. The Soviet Government demands the immediate cessation of the arbitrary measures taken by the Chinese authorities and directed against the Soviet Embassy in Peking, and demands freedom of movement for the members of the Embassy staff. Unless this is done within the shortest space of time, the Soviet side reserves the right to take necessary measures in reply."

The Soviet Government on the same day unilaterally cancelled the agreement allowing Chinese and Soviet citizens to visit each other's countries without a visa. Similar action was taken by the Chinese Government on Feb. 10.

The siege of the Soviet Embassy, and particularly the assaults on women and children, aroused intense indignation in the Soviet Union, where protest meetings were held in many cities. Delegations visited the Chinese Embassy in Moscow daily from Feb. 6–9 with protest resolutions, and when the Embassy refused to accept them posted them up nearby. On Feb. 7 the Embassy admitted one delegation which had been waiting for an hour, and afterwards protested to the Soviet Foreign Ministry that they had forcibly broken into the Embassy.

At a public meeting in Peking on Feb. 11 Chou En-lai violently denounced the Soviet "revisionists" but said that no reprisals should be taken against Soviet diplomats. His speech was broadcast but was not published in the Press. On Feb. 12, however, the Soviet Embassy staff were informed that they could now leave the building, "provided they did not provoke incidents," and the demonstrations outside the Embassy came to an end.

In an analysis of the reasons for the demonstrations, published on Feb. 10, *Le Monde* said: "In the eyes of the small Cultural Revolution Group around Mao Tse-tung, it is above all a question of consolidating internal unity against a 'foreign threat' from the Soviet Union, at a time when resistance to the excesses of the 'Revolutionary Rebels' threatens to assume increased proportions and even to develop into civil war in border regions such as Sinkiang, Tibet, Manchuria, and Yunnan. Some East European diplomats regard Kang Sheng (a former official of the Comintern in Moscow from 1933–35 and a specialist in relations with the former fraternal parties) as the most determined supporter of a complete break with the 'revisionist' Socialist camp. . . . Chou En-lai, on the other hand, seems to represent a slightly more moderate viewpoint, and to be seeking to avoid the worst. Apart from internal reasons, the campaign against the Soviet Union may be motivated by the following considerations:

"(1) The necessity to end the few remaining contacts between the Russians and their last Chinese informants. . . . Until recently the Soviet diplomats were better informed than any of their colleagues on certain events occurring even outside Peking. The affair of Yang Shang-kun, the former alternate member of the party secretariat accused by Red Guard papers of passing on party documents to the Russians, and even installing microphones in Mao Tse-tung's residence, may have played a determining role in the decision to provoke a break.

"(2) The prospect, now considered almost inevitable, of an international Communist conference in the near future makes it useless in Peking's eyes to preserve even the appearance of organic unity, and it is now a question only of finding ways of making Moscow bear the responsibility for the final break. The support given to 'revisionism' last year by the Japanese Communist Party, one of the last to remain faithful to the Peking line, is generally thought to have contributed to convince Mao that all consideration for foreign parties was useless.

"(3) The desire to dissociate China in advance from any eventual settlement of the Vietnamese war. . . ."

The Chinese Foreign Ministry on March 11 declared two Second Secretaries of the Soviet Embassy *personae non gratae,* on the ground that they had dismissed Chinese employees of the Embassy who had gone on strike in protest against the Moscow incident of Jan. 25; this "political persecution" was described as "extreme contempt of Chinese law and a gross insult to the working class of China." The Soviet Government expelled a First Secretary and a Third Secretary of the Chinese Embassy on March 18, accusing them of having organized the Embassy's anti-Soviet activities. *Le Monde* stated on March 25 that both the Chinese and the Soviet Press had shown restraint in their reports of the expulsion of the two Chinese diplomats, and commented that "since Chou En-lai's speech of Feb. 11 a sort of tacit agreement not to envenom relations further seems to have been reached."

Soviet Denunciation of Mao Tse-tung and Cultural Revolution (February–May 1967)

Following the siege of the Soviet Embassy in Peking, the Soviet Press published a series of fierce attacks on Mao Tse-tung and his policies from February onwards, the most important of which was a long analysis of the Cultural Revolution published in *Pravda* on Feb. 16, 1967.

"There is no longer any doubt," *Pravda* stated, "that the desire to divert the Chinese people's attention from the privations and difficulties which they are enduring, and the many mistakes and failures in China's internal and foreign policies, is one of the immediate causes of the present Chinese leadership's anti-Soviet policy and propaganda. It is no accident that they fired the first shots in their political war against the Soviet State and party shortly after the failure of the 'Great Leap Forward' policy and the people's communes of unhappy memory. . . . Soon afterwards purely nationalist and even racialist elements had already become obvious in Chinese propaganda. . . . By making the Chinese people believe that they are surrounded by enemies on all sides, the leaders in Peking are trying to organize them on a nationalist basis. They wish to divert the workers' attention from the real problems facing the country and justify the military and bureaucratic dictatorship of Mao Tse-tung and his group. . . .

"Following the economic adventures launched by Mao Tse-tung, the Chinese leadership was forced practically to renounce economic planning and the construction of the material and technical basis of Socialism, and openly to abandon a policy aimed at raising the workers' living standards. In these conditions the rulers in Peking could only make a virtue of necessity by proclaiming that economic construction and the raising of living standards were 'anti-Socialist' and 'bourgeois.' . . . As the practice of world Socialism completely contradicts these ideas, the Chinese leaders have launched a campaign of calumnies against the Soviet Union and the other Socialist countries, describing their struggle for economic progress and the raising of the people's material and cultural standards as 'revisionism,' 'economism,' and even 'restoration of capitalism.' . . .

"Faced with growing opposition to their policy, they have launched an unprecedented campaign of massive reprisals against those with different ideas. It is understandable that the whole practice of the Soviet party and the other Communist parties, which consistently develop the Leninist norms of party life, strengthen the principles of collective leadership, and strictly insist on democratic principles in the activities of all party organizations from top to bottom, represents a danger to Mao Tse-tung and his power. For a long time Mao Tse-tung's group have been acting against their own party. The most elementary norms and principles—election of party organs, reports from the leaders to the party and its organizations, open discussion of the party line, etc.—are trampled upon in China. The personality cult of Mao Tse-tung is pushed to the point of absurdity and idolatry.

"The destruction of the party organizations and the persecution and extermination of party militants are now being carried on under the banner of the 'Cultural Revolution' by Mao Tse-tung's shock troops, with the support of the Army and the security organs. To justify all this and silence the Chinese Communists, who cannot help comparing what is happening in their country with the practice of other Communist parties, Mao Tse-tung's group needs to blacken the Leninist line of the Soviet party with absurd accusations of 'revisionism.' The history of the working-class movement shows that renegades from Marxism have always felt a fierce hatred for the flag which they have betrayed. Mao Tse-tung's group is no exception. One of the principal aims of the anti-Soviet hysteria which they are stirring up is to cut off the Chinese people from authentic Marxism-Leninism and the experience of world Socialism. Today this experience is not only foreign to the Chinese leaders but dangerous to them, for a knowledge of it could only show the Chinese Communist Party and people how far their leaders have departed from the interests of the revolution and of Socialism. . . .

"The actions of Mao Tse-tung's group are dictated not by strength but by weakness, by fear of the party and the people. Recent events have shown that the leaders in Peking have good reason to fear. The 'Cultural Revolution' has revealed the extent of the discontent which has spread among the workers, peasants, and intellectuals and even infiltrated into the Army and the young people, on whom Mao Tse-tung's group have relied. The events which have taken place under the banner of the 'Cultural Revolution' in reality have developed into a bitter struggle for power by Mao Tse-tung and his collaborators. Their policy shows that to keep power they are ready to sacrifice everything—the interests of Socialism, the interests of their people, and the interests of the revolution. . . ."

Other articles published in the Soviet Press during the next two months described Mao Tse-tung as a "megalomaniac"; *Izvestia* accused him of practising "cultural genocide" against the national minorities in China, while the *Literaturnaya Gazeta* said that Mao "thinks of creating something like a racialist *Reich* in Asia and even outside it."

Moscow Radio increased its Chinese broadcasts to 84 hours a week, and a second station, "Radio Peace and Progress," which had previously broadcast only in European languages, began broadcasting in Chinese on March 1. Both stations made violent attacks on Mao and his closest supporters, such as Marshal Lin Piao and Kang Sheng, whose hands were said to be "dripping with the blood of thousands of Communists whom he has tortured and shot." The Chinese radio retaliated by sending out propaganda broadcasts in Russian almost continuously for 22 hours every day.

Pravda's correspondent in Peking was ordered on May 6 to leave China within seven days, on the ground that he had "slandered the Cultural Revolution, the Chinese people and Mao Tse-tung."

The "Svirsk" Incident—Attack on Soviet Embassy in Peking (June–August 1967)

The Tass Agency reported on June 13 that the Soviet Foreign Ministry had recently protested to the Chinese Embassy in Moscow against hostile actions by Red Guards against Soviet diplomats, demanding that measures should be taken to ensure the necessary conditions for their normal work and safety. Despite this protest, while visiting Shenyang [Mukden] on business two members of the Soviet trade mission were attacked on June 17 by Red Guards, who accused them of collecting information about the Cultural Revolution and staged a "trial" of them. To a Soviet protest of June 21 the Chinese Foreign Ministry replied on July 3 with a counterprotest against the "stealing of intelligence" by Soviet diplomats.

Another serious incident occurred on Aug. 10, when the port authorities at Tailien [Dairen] alleged that the second officer of a Soviet merchant ship, the *Svirsk,* had not only refused to accept a badge bearing a portrait of Mao Tse-tung but had thrown it into the sea. The ship was prevented from sailing, and when the captain went ashore for clearance papers on the following day he was arrested, while Red Guards overran the ship and painted anti-Soviet slogans. Although a Soviet Note demanded the captain's immediate release and the ship's unhindered departure, the captain was paraded through the streets in a lorry on Aug. 12, and a mob again invaded the ship, blocking the funnel, tearing down the aerial, and breaking other equipment. After Mr. Kosygin had sent a telegram to Chou En-lai, warning him that these "arbitrary and lawless acts" were "placing in doubt the fulfilment of existing trade relations between the Soviet Union and China," the *Svirsk* was allowed to sail on Aug. 13; a Chinese Note of the same date asserted that its crew had been instructed to insult Mao Tse-tung while in port, and that it had therefore been decided to "deport" the captain and conduct the ship out of Chinese waters.

A Soviet Note of Aug. 20 recalled that in addition to the *Svirsk* incident, another Soviet ship had been detained at Tailien for 20 days under a pretext in December 1966, and stated that two others had been forced to sail from the port on Aug. 15 without taking on cargo. These incidents, the Note declared, "place in question the implementation of the trade and navigation agreements . . . as in these abnormal conditions Soviet ships are unable to enter the port."

Protest demonstrations against the *Svirsk* incident began outside the Soviet Embassy in Peking on Aug. 14 and culminated in an attack on the building on Aug. 17, when Red Guards smashed windows, destroyed furniture and documents, beat up a Soviet diplomat, and set fire to an embassy car. A Soviet Note of Aug. 18 denounced the attack as "a great provocation, premeditated, organized, and carried out by the Mao Tse-tung group," and as a criminal act "incompatible with normal relations between States."

Celebrations of 50th Anniversary of Bolshevik Revolution (November 1967)

The celebrations of the 50th anniversary of the Bolshevik Revolution, held in Moscow in November, were attended by delegations from all the Communist countries except China, which had ignored an invitation, and Albania. At a joint session of the Supreme Soviets of the U.S.S.R. and the Russian Federation and the Communist Party central committee held on Nov. 3–4 Mr. Brezhnev criticized "the ideological and political degradation of some of the leaders of the Communist Party of China"; praised "the stubborn struggle waged by the finest sons of the Communist Party in China and by the progressive forces of the Chinese people to preserve the gains of Socialism"; and declared that "the attitude of Mao Tse-tung's group hampers co-ordinated assistance to Vietnam from all Socialist countries." At this point Chinese diplomats walked out of the meeting.

At a mass meeting in Peking on Nov. 6 Marshal Lin Piao denounced the Soviet leaders as "accomplices of U.S. imperialism" who had betrayed the revolution and restored capitalism. An editorial published on the same day in the *People's Daily, Liberation Army Daily,* and *Red Flag* described them as "renegades to the October Revolution," and claimed that the Cultural Revolution represented "the third great milestone in the history of the development of Marxism."

Chinese Reaction to Soviet Invasion of Czechoslovakia (August 1968)

Soviet forces, together with Polish, Hungarian, East German, and Bulgarian units, invaded Czechoslovakia during the night of Aug. 20–21, 1968, with the object of suppressing Mr. Dubcek's liberal Communist regime. Chou En-lai described the invasion on Aug. 23 as "the most barefaced and typical specimen of Fascist power politics played by the Soviet revisionist clique against its so-called allies," and declared: "The Chinese Government and people strongly condemn the Soviet revisionist clique and its followers for their crime of aggression, and firmly support the Czechoslovak people in their heroic resistance struggle against the Soviet occupation. . . The Soviet revisionist clique of renegades has long since degenerated into a gang of social-imperialists and social-Fascists." At the same time, Chinese statements strongly denounced Mr. Dubcek's regime both for its "revisionism" and for its failure to organize armed resistance to the invasion.

The Theory of "Limited Sovereignty"— Marshal Lin Piao's Reply (November 1968–April 1969)

Addressing the Polish United Workers' Party congress on Nov. 12, Mr. Brezhnev attempted to justify the invasion of Czechoslovakia by putting forward the so-called theory of "limited sovereignty," i.e. that when internal developments in a Communist country endangered "the Socialist community as a whole" other Communist countries were justified in intervening.

After insisting that Communist countries stood for strict respect for sovereignty, Mr. Brezhnev continued: "But when internal and external forces that are hostile to Socialism try to turn the development of some Socialist country towards the restoration of a capitalist regime, when Socialism in that country and the Socialist community as a whole is threatened, it becomes not only a problem of the country concerned, but a common problem and concern of all Socialist countries. Naturally, an action such as military assistance to a fraternal country designed to avert the threat to the social system is an extraordinary step, dictated by necessity." Such a step, he added, "may be taken only in case of direct actions of the enemies of Socialism within a country and outside it, actions threatening the common interests of the Socialist camp."

Although Mr. Brezhnev's doctrine was one which the Soviet Government had already applied in Hungary in 1956 at Chinese instigation, it was strongly denounced in China, presumably because it could be used to justify Soviet intervention in that country. Marshal Lin Piao commented on the theory on April 1, 1969, in his report to the ninth congress of the Chinese Communist Party, and prophesied that the Soviet Government would be overthrown by its own people.

"Since Brezhnev came to power," he said, "with its baton becoming less and less effective and its difficulties at home and abroad growing more and more serious, the Soviet revisionist renegade clique has been practising social-

106

imperialism and social-Fascism more frantically than ever. Internally, it has intensified its suppression of the Soviet people and speeded up the all-round restoration of capitalism. Externally, it has stepped up its collusion with U.S. imperialism and its suppression of the revolutionary struggles of the people of various countries, intensified its control over and its exploitation of various East European countries and the People's Republic of Mongolia, intensified its contention with U.S. imperialism over the Middle East and other regions, and intensified its threat of aggression against China . . .

"In order to justify its aggression and plunder, the Soviet revisionist renegade clique trumpets the so-called theory of 'limited sovereignty,' the theory of 'international dictatorship,' and the theory of 'Socialist community.' What does all this stuff mean? It means that your sovereignty is 'limited,' while his is unlimited. You won't obey him? He will exercise 'international dictatorship' over you—dictatorship over the people of other countries, in order to form the 'Socialist community' ruled by the new tsars . . . We firmly believe that the proletariat and the broad masses of the people in the Soviet Union, with their glorious revolutionary tradition, will surely rise and overthrow this clique consisting of a handful of renegades."

In another passage of his report, in which he reaffirmed the party's views on the inevitability of war, Marshal Lin Piao opposed the "social-imperialist" countries (i.e. the U.S.S.R.) to the Socialist countries (i.e. China and Albania), and suggested that a conflict existed in the former between the proletariat and the "bourgeoisie," implying that the U.S.S.R. had ceased to be a Socialist country.

"Lenin pointed out, imperialism means war," he said. " 'Imperialist wars are absolutely inevitable under such an economic system, as long as private property in the means of production exists.' Lenin further pointed out: 'Imperialist war is the eve of Socialist revolution.' These scientific theses of Lenin's are by no means out of date.

"Chairman Mao has recently pointed out: 'With regard to the question of world war, there are but two possibilities; one is that the war will give rise to revolution, and the other is that revolution will prevent the war.' This is because there are four major contradictions in the world today: the contradiction between the oppressed nations on the one hand and imperialism and social-imperialism on the other; the contradiction between the proletariat and the bourgeoisie in the capitalist and revisionist countries; the contradiction between imperialist and social-imperialist countries and among the imperialist countries; and the contradiction between Socialist countries on the one hand and imperialism and social-imperialism on the other. The existence and development of these contradictions are bound to give rise to revolution. According to the historical experience of World War I and World War II, it can be said with certainty that if the imperialists, revisionists, and reactionaries should impose a third world war on the people of the world, it would only greatly accelerate the development of these contradictions and help arouse the people of the world to rise in revolution and send the whole pack of imperialists, revisionists, and reactionaries to their graves."

VII: FRONTIER DISPUTES AND ARMED CLASHES, 1960–69

The Sino-Soviet frontier falls into two sections, divided by the buffer State of Outer Mongolia: the Central Asian sector, which divides the Chinese province of Sinkiang from the Soviet Republics of Tajikistan, Kirghizia, and Kazakhstan, and the Far Eastern sector, which divides Manchuria from north-eastern Siberia. From the 18th century onwards the Russian frontier in Central Asia was pushed steadily eastwards from Lake Balkhash, and large areas formerly under Chinese suzerainty were annexed in 1864 and 1881. Under the Kuomintang regime and for some years after the Communist revolution in China, Chinese maps of the region laid claim to large areas of Soviet territory, and more recent maps showed as "undefined" sections of the frontier which the U.S.S.R. regarded as final. Before the Chinese Communist revolution the Soviet Government actively encouraged anti-Chinese movements in Sinkiang, where the majority of the population are non-Chinese; after a revolt against the local Chinese administration, which was driven out, an "East Turkestan Republic" was established under Soviet protection in 1944 in the Ili region, which has a population of over 1,000,000, and was reintegrated into Sinkiang only after 1949. Although at least 2,000,000 Chinese have been settled in Sinkiang since 1949, the majority of the population still consists of Kazakhs, Tajiks, Kirghiz, Uighurs, and Uzbeks—the same peoples which form the majority of the population in the adjacent Soviet Republics.

In the Far East the sparsely populated wastelands north of the Amur and east of the Ussuri became part of the Chinese Empire in the 17th century as a result of the Manchu conquest of China, but were never effectively settled by the Chinese. The Treaty of Aigun (1858), which was imposed on China by the Tsarist Government at a time when that country had been weakened by a war with Britain and France in 1856–58, gave Russia sovereignty over 230,000 square miles north of the River Amur and placed 150,000 square miles east of the Ussuri (the Amur's principal tributary) under joint Sino-Russian control. The Treaty of Peking (1860) incorporated the territory east of the Ussuri into the Russian Empire, which later founded the port and city of Vladivostok on the newly acquired territory.

(Reprinted, with permission, from *The Times*, London

109

The "unequal treaties," as well as others recognizing Russian spheres of influence and extra-territorial rights in China, were intensely resented by the Chinese. After the Russian Revolution the Soviet Government proclaimed on Sept. 27, 1920, that it "declares null and void all the treaties concluded with China by the former Governments of Russia, renounces all seizure of Chinese territory and all Russian concessions in China, and restores to China, without any compensation and for ever, all that had been predatorily seized from her by the Tsar's Government and the Russian bourgeoisie." An agreement with China signed in 1924 repudiated all unequal and secret treaties with China, and renounced all Russian spheres of influence, extra-territorial rights, and consular jurisdiction in China, but did not deal with frontier questions.

The boundary question, which had been in abeyance since the Communist revolution in China, again came to the fore as relations between the two countries deteriorated. Later statements from both Soviet and Chinese sources revealed that border incidents began on July 1, 1960, after the recall of Soviet technicians from China, although no publicity was given to them at the time. In his speech of April 1, 1969, Marshal Lin Piao stated that China had proposed to the Soviet Government on Aug. 22 and Sept. 21, 1960, that negotiations should be held to settle the boundary question.

Boundary Question raised by China (1963)

The possibility of a revision of the frontiers was first mentioned publicly by China in March 1963, in response to a passage in Mr. Khrushchev's speech of Dec. 12, 1962, in which when defending his policy during the Cuban crisis he referred to China's attitude towards former Chinese territory annexed by Western Powers.

"One must be very cautious," Mr. Khrushchev declared, "and not rush in with irresponsible charges such as that some pursue an orthodox and others a mistaken policy, some are attacking imperialism while others tolerate it." After ironically contrasting the expulsion of the Portuguese from Goa by India with the Chinese Government's omission to take similar action against Macao and Hong Kong, he continued: "The odour coming from these places is by no means sweeter than that which was released by colonialism in Goa. But no one will denounce China for leaving these fragments of colonialism intact. It would be wrong to prod China into actions which she considers untimely. If the Chinese Government tolerates Macao and Hong Kong, it clearly has good

110

reasons for doing so. It would therefore be ridiculous to levy against it the accusation that these are concessions to the British and Portuguese colonialists, that this is appeasement. . . ."

In reply to this remark, the *People's Daily* mentioned on March 8, 1963, nine treaties which former Chinese Governments had been forced to sign, including the Treaties of Aigun and Peking, and inquired: "In raising questions of this kind do you intend to raise all the questions of unequal treaties and invite a general settlement?" This comment was interpreted as a suggestion that China reserved the right to demand the return of these territories at some future date.

A Soviet Government statement issued on Sept. 21 alleged that the Chinese had "systematically violated" the Soviet border, and that Chinese propaganda was demanding the revision of the frontier.

"Since 1960," the statement said, "Chinese servicemen and civilians have been systematically violating the Soviet border. In the single year 1960 over 5,000 violations of the Soviet border from the Chinese side were recorded. Attempts are also being made to 'develop' some parts of Soviet territory without permission." The statement went on to quote a document, allegedly issued by the Chinese administration in Manchuria, instructing fishermen to ignore orders by Soviet border guards to keep off disputed islands in the Amur and the Ussuri.

"The Soviet Government," the statement continued, "has invited the Chinese Government a number of times to hold consultations on the question of ascertaining separate sections of the border line, to exclude any possibility of misunderstanding. The Chinese side, however, evades such consultations while continuing to violate the border. This cannot but make us wary, especially in view of the fact that Chinese propaganda is making definite hints at the 'unjust demarcation' of some sections of the Soviet-Chinese border allegedly made in the past. However, the artificial creation of any territorial problems in our times, especially between Socialist countries, would be tantamount to embarking on a very dangerous path. . . ."

Tension on Central Asian Border (1963)

Chinese and Soviet statements issued in September indicated that a tense situation existed on the Sinkiang border.

The *People's Daily* alleged on Sept. 6 that Soviet agencies and personnel had carried out "large-scale subversive activities in the Ili region of Sinkiang and incited and coerced several tens of thousands of Chinese citizens into going to the Soviet Union." In an interview with the Soviet newspaper *Komsomolskaya Pravda,* published on Sept. 20, 1963, four refugees from Sinkiang stated that the Chinese attitude to such peoples as the Kazakhs and Kirghiz had greatly deteriorated, especially if they claimed Soviet citizenship, and that about 400 officials who sympathized with the Soviet Union had been sent to a labour camp.

According to reports from Moscow, riots had occurred in Sinkiang in recent years among the Moslem Kazakhs, Uighurs, and other nationalities, who resented Chinese attempts to suppress their religion and languages, and between the middle of 1962 and September 1963 about 50,000 Kazakhs and other tribesmen had fled into the U.S.S.R.

Boundary Negotiations—Further Controversy over Frontiers (1964–66)

Boundary negotiations began in Peking on Feb. 25, 1964, but were suspended in the following May without any progress having been achieved. According to Soviet sources, the Soviet delegation put forward proposals for the "clarification" of certain sections of the border, but the Chinese delegation laid claim to over 1,500,000 square kilometres (580,000 square miles) of Soviet territory, whilst stating that China would not press her claims for the present. According to the Chinese version, the Chinese delegation, while regarding the Treaties of Aigun and Peking as "unequal treaties," offered to take them as a basis for determining the entire alignment of the boundary, subject to "necessary readjustments at individual places on the boundary by both sides," but the Soviet delegation refused to accept these proposals. Although it was agreed in principle to resume the talks in Moscow at a later date, no further negotiations took place.

The controversy was revived by an interview given by Mao Tse-tung on July 10 to a group of Japanese Socialists, at which he was reported to have said: "There are too many places occupied by the Soviet Union. . . Some people have said that Sinkiang province and the territory north of the Amur River must be included in the Soviet Union. The U.S.S.R. is concentrating troops on its border. . . China has not yet asked the Soviet Union for an account about Vladivostok, Khabarovsk, Kamchatka, and other towns and regions east of Lake Baikal, which became Russian territory about 100 years ago."

Pravda printed the Mao Tse-tung interview on Sept. 2, together with a long editorial which gave warning that any attempt to enforce the Chinese territorial claims could have "the most dangerous consequences."

The *Pravda* editorial said: "We are faced with an openly expansionist programme with far-reaching pretensions. This programme did not appear to-day or yesterday. In 1954 a text-book on modern history was published in China with a map showing China as it was, in the authors' opinion, before the First Opium War. This map included Burma, Vietnam, Korea, Thailand, Malaya, Nepal, Bhutan, and Sikkim in China. In the north the border ran along the Stanovik mountain range, cutting off the Maritime Territory from the U.S.S.R. In the west a part of Kirghizia, Tajikistan, and Kazakhstan up to Lake Balkhash were included in China. Sakhalin was also shown as Chinese. If one is to believe the text-book, all these lands and countries were 'State territory of China' and had been taken away from it . . .

"By what right do the Chinese leaders lay claim to territories which have never belonged to China? They refer to the fact that centuries ago Chinese troops passed through these territories and Chinese emperors sometimes collected tribute from the population. If the problem were not so serious, so-called historical arguments of the type used by Mao Tse-tung could only be described as childish. . . . Do those who question the Soviet Union's possession of a territory of more than 1,500,000 square kilometres think how these claims will be taken by Soviet people who have been living and working on this land for several generations and regard it as their homeland? . . ."

In conclusion, *Pravda* declared that "any attempt to re-carve the map of the world" could lead to "the most dangerous consequences."

In an interview with a Japanese delegation on Sept. 15, Mr. Khrushchev replied to Mao Tse-tung's statements by advocating self-determination for the non-Chinese peoples of Sinkiang and Inner Mongolia.

"Mao Tse-tung," said Mr. Khrushchev, "has declared that the Soviet Union is too large and that Tsarist Russia conquered too much Chinese territory. I have no wish to defend Tsarism; the Tsars and the Chinese Emperors were much the same. But the Chinese Emperors conquered Inner Mongolia, Man-churia, Tibet, and Sinkiang. Sinkiang is not China; Kazakhs and Uighurs live there. The bulk of the Kazakhs and Kirghiz live in Soviet Kazakhstan and Kirghizia, but there are also Kazakhs, Kirghiz, and even Uzbeks in Sinkiang. So, too, the independent State of Mongolia contains only half the Mongol people. The other half lives in China. Mao Tse-tung wishes to settle political questions not on a political but on an ethnographical basis. If questions are to be discussed on that basis, we do not lack arguments. Kazakhstan must decide its own destiny. We support self-determination. The Chinese must do the same. . . ."

In its letter sent early in 1966 to other Communist parties (see Chapter V) the Soviet party accused China of "provoking border conflicts." In reply to this allegation Marshal Chen Yi accused the U.S.S.R. on May 20 of provoking over 5,000 incidents between July 1960 and the end of 1965, of concentrating troops on the Chinese frontier, and of conducting military manoeuvres which presupposed that China was the enemy.

Incidents during the Cultural Revolution (1966–68)

The tension on the borders greatly increased during the earlier stages of the Cultural Revolution.

It was reported from Moscow on Oct. 2, 1966, that 2,000,000 Chinese were estimated to have taken part in mass demonstations on the Soviet frontier in support of China's territorial claims, especially on the border between Manchuria and the Soviet Far East, and that Chinese troops had opened fire several times on Soviet ships plying on the River Amur. In view of the strained situation, military training schools were reported on Dec. 7 to have been established for the civilian population in the Soviet Republics of Kazakhstan, Tajikistan, and Kirghizia.

The situation became particularly tense during the siege of the Soviet Embassy in February 1967. Peking Radio alleged on Feb. 2 that a plot by the "Soviet revisionists and U.S. and Japanese imperialists" to attack China through Heilungkiang province (Manchuria) had been smashed, and on Feb. 11 all Chinese frontier troops were placed on the alert. On the following day wall newspapers in Peking alleged that a company of the Chinese Army had recently repulsed an attack by a Soviet battalion near Vladivostok, taking a number of prisoners; this report was not confirmed by any other source.

Western sources estimated the number of troops on the Sino-Soviet border at this time at nearly 40 Soviet divisions, many of which had recently been transferred from Eastern Europe, and between 50 and 60 Chinese divisions, or more than 600,000 men. It was reported from Moscow on Feb. 21, however, that except for frontier guards all Chinese troops had been withdrawn about 100 miles from the Soviet and Mongolian borders, creating a "no man's land" from which all civilians had been evacuated.

The Soviet Press reported in January that several hundred thousand Uighurs and Kazakhs had crossed the border from Sinkiang in recent months and taken refuge in the Soviet Union; this exodus was attributed to fear of the Cultural Revolution and the hunt for Soviet sympathizers which accompanied it, the mass settlement of

114

Chinese in Sinkiang, and the alleged persecution of national minorities. The evacuation of civilians from the frontier areas was reported on Feb. 21 to have been particularly thorough in Sinkiang, with the result that the flight of refugees into the Soviet Union had been almost brought to an end.

According to diplomatic sources in Moscow, many minor incidents took place in 1968, but neither side gave them any publicity; a Chinese protest Note of Sept. 16, 1968, however, alleged that Soviet military aircraft had flown over Heilungkiang province 29 times between Aug. 9 and 29.

The Damansky Island Fighting (March 1969)

Armed clashes between Soviet and Chinese frontier guards, causing considerable loss of life, occurred on March 2 and March 15 on the River Ussuri. The scene of the fighting was a small uninhabited island 1½ miles long by half a mile wide, known to the Russians as Damansky Island and to the Chinese as Chenpao Island, which lies about 110 miles south of Khabarovsk and 250 miles north of Vladivostok.

The status of the island under the Treaties of Aigun and Peking is disputed.

A Chinese Foreign Ministry statement of March 10 contended that under international law the central line of the main channel of the Ussuri formed the boundary line, that the island was situated on the Chinese side of this line, and that it had always been under Chinese jurisdiction and had been admitted to be Chinese by the Soviet delegation at the boundary negotiations in 1964. A Soviet Note of March 29 [see page 119], on the other hand, maintained that a map approved by both Governments in 1861 showed the Chinese bank of the Ussuri as the boundary line in this area. The problem was complicated by the fact that after the breaking up of the ice in spring the Ussuri regularly floods its banks and frequently shifts its channel.

The Chinese statement of March 10 asserted that Soviet frontier troops had intruded into "the Chenpao Island area of China" 16 times between Jan. 23, 1967, and March 2, 1969, wounding Chinese frontier guards on several occasions, whilst Major-General Vasily Lobanov (Soviet commander in the Pacific frontier district) claimed on March 16 that Chinese troops had repeatedly attempted to capture the island during the past 18 months.

Diametrically opposite accounts of the clash on March 2 were given by the two sides. According to the Soviet version, about 300 Chinese soldiers, camouflaged in white cloaks, crossed the frozen river during the night of March 1–2 to Damansky Island, where they lay in ambush. In the morning about 30 more Chinese approached the island and, when Soviet frontier guards came up to them to protest, opened fire without warning. At the same time both the troops on the island and others on the Chinese bank of the river opened fire with rifles and artillery on another group of Soviet frontier guards. With the help of reinforcements from a neighbouring post, it was stated, the Soviet troops had expelled the intruders after a two-hour battle, in which they had lost 31 killed, including an officer, and 14 wounded. Chinese official statements, on the other hand, stated that a large Soviet force, accompanied by four armoured vehicles, had opened fire on Chinese frontier guards who were on normal patrol duty, killing and wounding many of them.

Both Governments sent strongly worded protest Notes to the other on March 2. The Soviet Note demanded an immediate investigation, the punishment of those responsible for the incident, and immediate steps to preclude any further violation of the frontier, and declare that "reckless and provocative actions by the Chinese authorities" would be "met on our side by a rebuff." The Chinese Note similarly demanded the punishment of the culprits, reserved the right to demand compensation, and declared that if the Soviet Government continued to "provoke armed conflicts" it would receive "resolute counter-blows."

Mass protest demonstrations began on March 3 outside the Soviet Embassy in Peking, which for four days was virtually besieged by thousands of Chinese servicemen and civilians shouting such slogans as "Hang Kosygin" and "Fry Brezhnev." Similar demonstrations, in which according to the New China News Agency 260,000,000 people took part, were held in the next few days throughout China. On the Russian side, although demonstrations took place in Khabarovsk and Vladivostok on March 3–4, there were no demonstrations in Moscow until March 7, when over 50,000 people marched past the Chinese Embassy in the largest organized protest seen in the city for many years; some of the crowd threw stones, lumps of ice, ink bottles, and paint bombs at the building, and many windows were broken.

116

At a press conference on March 7 Mr. Leonid Zamyatin (head of the Soviet Foreign Ministry press department), after giving the first detailed account of the incident, alleged that the Chinese had shot and bayoneted wounded men, and that the faces of some of those killed had been "so mutilated as to be unrecognizable." An even larger demonstration than that of the previous day occurred outside the Chinese Embassy in Moscow on March 8, over 100,000 people taking part, although on this occasion there were no disorders; protest meetings were also held on March 8-9 in many other Russian cities. In Peking protest demonstrations against the stoning of the Chinese Embassy in Moscow began outside the Soviet Embassy on March 11, and continued for three days. *Red Flag* (the Chinese Communist Party's theoretical organ) declared on March 14 that if the Soviet leadership wanted to fight, "let us thoroughly annihilate them." The article added: "The Soviet revisionists have created such theories as 'limited sovereignty' to help Soviet troops march into other countries [i.e. Czechoslovakia]. This makes us understand that their recent armed provocation is no mere coincidence."

A Chinese Note of March 13, which the Soviet Embassy refused to accept, alleged that between March 4 and March 12 Soviet armoured vehicles had "intruded into China's territory, Chenpao Island," on six occasions, and that Soviet helicopters had twice flown over it during this period. Soviet official statements claimed that a group of Chinese soldiers had attempted to "invade" the island on March 14 but had been driven off.

Further fighting occurred on March 15, and was apparently on a much larger scale than that on March 2. General Lobanov told the Press on March 16 that Chinese infantry in regimental strength—or up to 2,000 men—had launched repeated attacks on the island under cover of artillery and mortar fire from the Chinese bank, and had been driven back, with the aid of frontier guards from neighbouring posts and the reserve, only after seven hours' fighting. According to the version given by Peking Radio, large numbers of Soviet troops supported by tanks repeatedly attacked the Chinese frontier guards on duty on the island, and were driven back after an 11-hour battle during which Soviet heavy artillery and tanks shelled the island and the Chinese bank of the river. Although neither side gave details of the casualties, these were evidently heavy; Soviet press reports mentioned by name 12 officers and n.c.o.s who had been killed, including a colonel, suggesting—according to the Moscow correspondent of *The Times*—that a full regiment of frontier guards and reserves, or nearly 3,000 men, had been engaged on the Soviet side.

Only minor incidents were subsequently reported from the area. The Soviet Press reported on several occasions between March 18 and April 8 that the Chinese had directed mortar and machine-gun fire against the island and were digging fortifications on their side of the river, whilst Peking Radio alleged on April 13 that the Russians had committed "new acts of aggression" on the Ussuri frontier, without giving any further details.

A Chinese Note of March 15 accused the Soviet Government of "incessantly" sending troops to intrude into Chinese territory, and demanded that it should immediately stop its "armed provocations." A Soviet Note of the same date maintained that "Damansky Island is an inalienable part of Soviet territory," and declared that "if further attempts are made to violate the inviolability of Soviet territory, the U.S.S.R. and all its peoples will resolutely defend it and will deliver a crushing rebuff to such violations."

For some days after the fighting on March 15 both the Chinese and the Soviet Press published virulent and bellicose attacks on the other country's leaders; the Peking *People's Daily* described "Khrushchev, Kosygin, Brezhnev, and company" on March 20 as "a herd of swine," asserting that the Soviet people hated "the new tsars," whilst the Soviet armed forces newspaper *Red Star* denounced Mao Tse-tung on March 23 as "a traitor to the sacred cause of Communism . . . painted with human blood" and compared him to Hitler. The fact that protest demonstrations were not resumed in either country, however, despite the seriousness of the latest fighting, suggested that both Governments were anxious not to push matters to extremes.

Soviet Proposals for Boundary Negotiations
(March–April 1969)

Mr. Kosygin asked on March 21 to communicate with the Chinese leaders by telephone. The Chinese Government replied on the following day with a memorandum stating that "in view of the present relations between China and the Soviet Union, it is unsuitable to communicate by telephone. If the Soviet Government has anything to say, it is asked to put it forward officially to the Chinese Government through diplomatic channels."

In a long and moderately worded Note of March 29 the Soviet

Government reaffirmed in detail its claim to sovereignty over Daman-sky Island, and proposed that the boundary negotiations broken off in 1964 should be resumed as soon as possible.

After giving the Soviet version of the incidents on March 2 and 15, the Note contended that the Chinese Government had signified its acceptance of the existing frontiers by concluding an agreement on shipping on the Amur and the Ussuri in 1951, and by asking the competent Soviet authorities for permission to use certain islands in those rivers for cutting hay and timber—an indication that they did not question the Soviet claim to those islands, including Damansky Island.

The Note went on to recall the friendly relations between the two countries in the 1950s, and commented: "If it were not for the position adopted by the Chinese side, trade, economic, and scientific and technical co-operation between our countries would undoubtedly have developed successfully further. This also holds true for today. . . . Whenever a danger arose to the security of the People's Republic of China, the Soviet Union, loyal to its commitments under the Treaty of Friendship, Alliance, and Mutual Assistance, always came out in support of People's China." [These statements were interpreted by Western observers as a suggestion that in the event of a change in Chinese policy the Soviet Union would be prepared to resume its economic aid and diplomatic support to China.]

After deploring the breaking off of boundary negotiations, and recalling that the Chinese Premier, Chou En-lai, had said in 1960 that the unestablished sections of the Soviet-Chinese frontier were "insignificant discrepancies in the maps, easy to solve peacefully," the Soviet Note urged the Chinese Government to "refrain from any actions on the frontier that may cause complications and to solve any differences that may arise in a calm atmosphere and through negotiations." It proposed that the consultations started in Peking in 1964 should be resumed as soon as possible, and concluded: "The Soviet Government is firmly convinced that in the final count the vital interests of the Soviet and Chinese peoples will make it possible to remove and overcome difficulties in Soviet-Chinese relations. The Soviet Government has stated, and considers it necessary to repeat, that it resolutely rejects any encroachments by anyone on Soviet territory, and that any attempts to talk to the Soviet Union and the Soviet people in the language of weapons will be firmly repulsed."

Marshal Lin Piao stated on April 1 that the Chinese Government was considering its reply to the Soviet Note. A second Soviet Note of April 11 proposed that the boundary negotiations should be resumed in Moscow on April 15 or at any other early date convenient for the Chinese.

(Sources: Soviet Embassy Press Department, London—*Peking Review*—*Times*, London—*Daily Telegraph*, London—*Guardian*, London—*Le Monde*, Paris—*New York Times*).

SELECT BIBLIOGRAPHY

CLEMENS, W. C., *The Arms Race and Sino-Soviet Relations,* Stanford University, Hoover Institute on War, Revolution and Peace, 1968.

CRANKSHAW, EDW., *The New Cold War; Moscow v. Peking,* Penguin, 1963.

GARTHOFF, R. L. (ed.), *Sino-Soviet Military Relations,* Praeger/Pall Mall Press, 1967.

GITTINGS, JOHN, Survey of the Sino-Soviet Dispute. A Commentary and Extracts from the Recent Polemics. Oxford University Press for the Royal Institute of International Affairs, 1969.

GRIFFITH, W. E., *Sino-Soviet Relations 1964–65,* M.I.T.P., 1967.

GRIFFITH, W. E., *Sino-Soviet Rift,* Library of International Studies Series, Allen and Unwin, 1964.

HALPERIN, M. H. (ed.), *Sino-Soviet Relations and Arms Control,* M.I.T.P., 1967.

HOUSTON, J. V. D., *Russia and China,* R. Hale, 1960.

JACKSON, W. A. D., *The Russo-Chinese Borderlands,* 2nd ed., Van Nostrand, 1968.

LABEDZ, LEOPOLD, and URBAN, G. (ed.), *The Sino-Soviet Conflict,* Background Books, The Bodley Head, 1965.

LEVINE, D. C., *The Rift: the Sino-Soviet Conflict,* Harris-Wolfe, 1968.

RUPEN, R. A. and FARRELL, R. (ed.), *Vietnam and the Sino-Soviet Dispute,* Praeger, 1967.

SALISBURY, HARRISON E., The Coming War between Russia and China. Secker & Warburg / Pan Books, 1969.

WEI, H., *China and Soviet Russia,* Van Nostrand, 1956.

WU, A. K., *China and the Soviet Union,* Kennicat, 1968.

ZAGORIA, D. S., *Sino-Soviet Conflict 1956–61,* Princeton, O.U.P., 1962.